FALL of the WEST ™

Written by John Lambshead

Front & Back Cover and Internal Colour Artwork by Michael Perry

Black & White Internal Artwork by Allessandro Pascoletti

Battle diagrams by Alan Perry & Michael Perry

Production Work by Talima Fox, Nick Davis & Adrian Wood   *Logo by Adrian Wood*

Figures painted by Jim Bowen, Ben Jefferson, Chris Adcock, Dave Thomas, Bruno Allanson, Aly Morrison, Keith Robertson, Alan Perry & Michael Perry

Armoured Roman Infantryman

All figures from **Foundry**

Buildings scratchbuilt by Alan Perry, Michael Perry & Nigel Stillman.

Other buildings by Monolith and Grendal.

Tea and sandwiches by Rick Priestley and Jervis Johnson

Front Cover: Scola Gentilium Seniorum at the Battle of Strasbourg – 357 AD

Back Cover: A member of the Iovii Iuniores Gallicani

·CONTENTS·

·INTRODUCTION·

'The Roman Empire is beheaded… all things born are doomed to die… but who would have believed that Rome would crumble?'

Eusebius Hieronymus (St. Jerome) c.342-420 AD

This book is an account of warfare in the last 126 years of the Western Roman Empire. It is specifically designed for the Warhammer Ancient Battles game system, but we hope it will be useful to all wargamers interested in this fascinating period. The authors are wargamers, not professional historians, so our work is based on the mainstream opinions of scholars. There is a reading list at the back of the book that includes the major sources we have used in our research. We give an acknowledgement where we have used a source almost exclusively for a section. Where academic views differ or information is absent, we have used our best judgement to fill in the gaps.

Military technology evolved at glacial speed in the ancient world. Nevertheless, the late Roman army differed in a number of ways from the late Republican and early Imperial periods. In the early Empire, the army fielded legionary and auxiliary infantry. Legionaries were armed with a heavy, short range javelin (*pilum*) and a curved body shield. Auxiliaries carried a large flat shield and throwing spears, which could also be used in hand-to-hand combat. The evidence is that both types of infantry wore armour in battle but *lorica segmentata* is normally associated with legions.

Weapon choice, as always, followed military function. Legionaries were heavy infantry who made up the decisive line of battle. They threw the armour piercing *pilum* as a short range, heavy shock weapon and then fought hand-to-hand with *gladius* short swords from behind their shields. Auxiliaries fought either in the line with spears or swords as support troops, or in a looser order where they could act as skirmishers and pursuit troops. By the 4th century, this distinction had disappeared and all Roman soldiers resembled auxiliaries. They were armed with a flat shield, threw missile weapons and used spears and long swords. The long sword could be used in an overhead, slashing attack – barbarians rarely wore helmets.

A controversial point is whether late Roman infantry used body armour. The current view is that metal armour was worn in the line of battle and wherever else appropriate. It was probably not needed when policing or for certain special operations where mobility was at a premium.

The traditional view is that cavalry became more important in this period but this opinion is not well substantiated by the evidence. Cavalry certainly could win battles, but this was also true for most pre-industrial eras. Infantry was still the predominant and decisive arm of battle in the late Empire.

There were also significant organisational changes in the army. Units were smaller, and split into border guards and mobile troops that were often stationed deeper within the Empire. Military experts debate the strategic significance of this change, using modern ideas and terminology such as 'mobile reserve' or 'defence-in-depth', but it is uncertain whether the Romans thought in these terms or whether the creation of mobile armies was a military or political decision. Whatever, there is no evidence that the border troops were any less effective soldiers than their mobile colleagues. Indeed, the status of units could change as the military situation demanded and Roman commanders seem to have regarded the border and mobile units as interchangeable.

The barbarians were much the same as they had always been. They were a disorganised but culturally homogeneous mass with little concept of nationality. The *Barbaricum* produced warriors, not soldiers, and their armies were essentially collections of warbands held together at the unit level by kinship and at the army level by the personality of the warlord. It is unlikely that there were delineated tribes with different weapons or tactics. Certainly local ecology influenced barbarian forces, as eastwards the terrain became more suitable for horse rearing and concomitantly cavalry featured more heavily in eastern barbarian armies.

Crossing the frontier

·THE·END·OF·THE·EMPIRE·

"The best known fact about the Roman Empire is that it declined and fell."

Starr

Like the death of the dinosaurs, the fall of the Western Empire is a dramatic tragedy that has captured the popular imagination. Each generation has painted its own fears, preoccupations and plain bigotry onto this rich canvas. Conservatives have pontificated portentously about 'immorality', 'taxation' and 'state socialism' while socialists have muttered darkly of 'class divisions' and 'financial inequality'.

Not to be outdone and quite unhampered by factual evidence or historical knowledge, scientists have enthusiastically entered the fray. Doctors plumped for a medical explanation and pointed the finger at the debilitating impact of lead pollution in the water supply while, astonishingly, soil scientists discovered soil erosion to be the critical factor. In recent years, our fears of environmental disaster have caused the Roman collapse to be interpreted in the light of sea level changes or comet strikes.

Professional historians, who are hampered by knowledge, have swayed between extremes. A modern work lists 210 separate cited reasons for the fall of the Empire. The traditional view can be summed up as the 'downhill all the way school'. The great Gibbon, himself, could be described as close to this group. It is certainly true that the Roman political system encouraged military dictatorship accompanied by constant rebellion and civil war. A variant is to turn the question on its head and declare the Roman Empire to be 'impossible' and wonder how it survived for so long. Brown's ingenious and influential 1971 book – *The World of Late Antiquity* denied that the Empire had fallen at all; it had merely changed and changed and, er, changed. It was partly in answer to this that Ferrill in 1986 published *The Fall of the Roman Empire* that emphatically described a military collapse.

Desperate assault

Any hypothesis for the fall of the West has to successfully incorporate the fact that the Eastern Empire prospered. So many of the weaknesses of Roman civilisation, although real enough, may be dismissed as primary causes in the loss of the Western Empire simply because they did not preclude the survival of the Byzantine civilisation (why is the Roman civilisation based on Constantinople called Byzantine anyway?).

The critical turning point in Rome's fortunes was probably the division of the Empire into two separate, mildly hostile states in 395 AD under the ineffectual boy emperors Honorius and Arcadius and their squabbling advisers. Up to two thirds of the Imperial revenues needed to pay the army came from the Eastern provinces. Yet the Western Empire had by far the longest frontier, facing dangerous northern barbarians. Two thirds of the army had been based in the west. A glance at a map reveals the vulnerability of the long Rhine and Danube *limes* (borders) as well as the indented coasts of Britain and Gaul. In short, the West lacked the economic resources to pay enough soldiers to defend its extended borders.

Geography gave Byzantine civilisation an additional advantage. If barbarians crossed the northern border they could devastate the Balkans but would soon run up against the impregnable (to barbarians) barrier of Constantinople. The fortified city prevented them from crossing the Bosphorus into the rich Asian and African provinces. In contrast, once the border was breached in the west only North Africa had any form of geographic protection and the Straits of Gibraltar lacked a mighty fortress to impede barbarian migrations. A large barbarian horde moving through the Western Empire searching for food and loot could devastate province after province, further wrecking the economic base needed to pay the army in a downward spiral of destruction. In the 5th century this more or less happened.

If in 395 AD, the throne had been seized by one of the great soldier emperors who had the resources of a united Romania, could the Western Empire have been saved? Britain, Gaul and possibly Spain were probably too vulnerable but it should have been possible to hold North Africa and even Italy. Justinian's reconquest of the West would have started from a firmer strategic base, with the long term acquisition of Spain and even Gaul possible. Such a reconstituted Empire might have been able to resist the challenge of Islam. If this had happened would the world be a different place today?

Some historians consider that the Roman Empire had to fall to allow the flowering of modern Western culture (if flowering is the right word, some would compare Western civilisation more to a *leylandii* tree). They may be right but it is worth reflecting that in 300 AD the cities, villas and forts of Roman Britain had piped-in fresh water for drinking and bathing, flushing toilets and central heating. After the fall of Rome, it took fifteen centuries for British civilisation to recreate such wonders.

·HISTORY·

'The priests and the people, without any respect of persons, were destroyed with fire and sword, nor was there any left to bury those who had been cruelly slaughtered.'

Bede, Historia Ecclesiastica Gentis Anglorum, c.673-735 AD

THE LATE FOURTH CENTURY

A significant event happened in around 350 AD, the Roman army ceased to build new roads in Britain and Gaul. Roads carried the army, administration and commerce from one side of the Empire to the other; they were the arteries of civilisation. Nothing was more indicative of Western Imperial decline than the end of road building.

As the second half of the 4th century began, the understandably paranoiac Constantius II had just survived a period of violent civil war to emerge as sole ruler of the Empire. Taking advantage of weakness and confusion, barbarians flooded across the Rhine intent on a little raping, looting and land grabbing. Even Cologne had fallen to some of the Franks. In response, the Emperor dispatched his nephew, Julian 'the Apostate', to Gaul. Julian proved a successful commander clearing the frontier of invaders and annihilating a barbarian army at the Battle of Strasbourg, 355 AD. Even so, Constantius was forced to personally campaign across the Rhine before leaving his army under the command of the magister militum Barbatio.

More barbarian attacks followed in a seemingly endless stream of battles and skirmishes. Constantius led an army in person against the Alamanni, the Sarmatians and King Araharius of the Quadi. Meanwhile, Julian attacked the Franks and Alamanni and sent a mobile detachment to rescue Britain from the Picts. With the support of the Gallic army, Julian rebelled and became Emperor in 361 AD when Constantius died of natural causes before he could crush his desperate nephew.

In 359 AD, Persia attacked Roman Mesopotamia, storming the key fortified city of Amida. In response, Julian assembled a huge army of 65,000 men at Antioch and invaded the Persian Empire in March, 363 AD. With a detachment of 35,000 men, he advanced down the Euphrates supported by a fleet of 1,000 boats. But the Emperor seemed to have lost contact with his second detachment of 30,000 men and this army achieved little. King Shapur wisely refused battle and adopted a scorched earth policy, harassing the struggling Roman expeditionary force with his superior cavalry.

The Persians engaged unsuccessfully at Maranga. Another attack was beaten off at Samarra but this time Julian was killed by a loose javelin. It is still debated which side was responsible, as the Apostate was the sworn enemy of Christianity! The expedition was a disaster and Shapur demanded the mighty fortress of Nisibis as ransom for the trapped Roman army. The new emperor, Jovian, lasted eight months before he died, apparently of carbon monoxide poisoning from a badly constructed bedside fire!

Another general, Valentinian I, took command of the Empire in 364 AD. Crude, boorish but highly effective, he was one of the great fighting emperors. Appointing his ineffectual brother Valens to rule the East, he rode west to chastise the Moors of North Africa, the Picts and Scots of Britain and the Alamanni on the Rhine. Barbarians all round the Western borders had been raiding and invading while the cream of the mobile army was bogged down in Persia. Valentinian set up his imperial capital in Trier and rebuilt the Western army. To facilitate this, he reduced the height requirement from 5' 10", which was tall for a Roman, to a more average 5' 7".

Under Valentinian, the mobile army swung into action in the grand old style, driving the barbarians before them like sheep before wolves. Then a new round of civil wars started as Procopius, a kinsman of Julian, captured the cities of Nicaea and Cyzicus. He was beaten by Valens' field army at the Battle of Nakolia in May, 366 AD. Another of Julian's relatives, Marcellus, was executed around this time while trying to raise a Gothic army. Valens was back, campaigning against barbarians on the Danube in 367 AD and 369 AD before turning east to thwart Persian ambitions. Then he began a series of actions against the rude Alamanni and Saxons while Theodosius took part of the Western army to Africa in 373 AD to put down another revolt. The Emperor then turned his attention to the barbarians on the Danube. Disastrously, in 375 AD he died of a stroke, incensed by the insolent attitude of delegates from the Quadi and Sarmatians. Rome had lost its great general just as she was about to be tested in the fire.

Valentinian was survived by his sixteen year old son Gratian who became Western emperor in his place. The troops on the Danube promptly rebelled and appointed their own emperor, Valentinian's four year old son Valentinian II. To buy off the rebels, Gratian appointed his young half brother co-ruler. The West needed a military strongman; it got two boy emperors.

A chain of disasters started when a race of barbarians, the fearsome Hun, swept out of the east in the early 370s AD and smashed into the Ostrogoths, who lived to the north-east of the Black Sea. The Ostrogoths fled westward and in turn bumped into the Visigoths. Two displaced Visigothic kings, Fritigern and Alavivus, requested entry into the Eastern Empire. Valens agreed, a strategically unwise decision, and 200,000 Visigoths crossed the border in 376 AD. Corrupt Roman officials exploited them cruelly and unmercifully. There were stories of vicious exploitation, robbery and rape. Finally, some Ostrogoths took advantage of the confusion to cross without permission. The magister Lupicinus attacked the Ostrogoths but managed to slaughter some of the disarmed Visigoths during a truce. Not surprisingly, the unfortunate Visigoths revolted in utter desperation.

5

In their rage, the Germans ravaged the area around Adrianople, taking by force the food that had been denied them, burning the farms and towns. Only the walled city kept them out despite several attempts to take the place by storm. Fritigern made his famous comment that '*he kept peace with walls*' and returned his warriors to plundering the countryside. This anecdote indicates how effective defended fortifications were against barbarians.

The inadequate Valens decided that the problem was grave enough to require a praesental army and concentrated troops from the Western and Eastern mobile armies in Constantinople. From 376 AD to 377 AD, in a series of clashes, they penned the Visigoths into Thrace but failed to eliminate them. Finally, Valens in 378 AD gathered a huge army and marched on Adrianople. Gratian was delayed in the west while he rebuffed an attack by an Alamannic army, commanded by Priarius, in an action at Argentaria. The rumour that the Western army was to be posted east was enough to spark barbarians inroads. Priarius was just a little previous in his timing. Finally, Gratian force marched east but the delay had wide ranging consequences for the Empire.

With his usual perspicacity, Valens decided to attack Fritigern's army without waiting any longer for Western reinforcement. Around 40,000 Roman soldiers were lost in the worst debacle since Cannae. Valens' body was never found. Subsequently, Fritigern made another attack on Adrianople but was once more beaten off by fugitives from the defeated Roman army using the city's artillery batteries.

'*Keeping peace with walls*', the cunning Fritigern resorted to a stratagem. He persuaded some Roman captives to desert. Goths then chased the deserters to the city gates in a piece of playacting. Once inside, the refugees were supposed to distract the defenders by setting fire to buildings while Fritigern launched another assault. The plot failed when suspicious city defenders placed the deserters under arrest.

Abandoning the siege, Fritigern marched on Constantinople, arguably the most heavily fortified city in the world. Not surprisingly, the Goths were repulsed in panic and disorder. After the failure at Adrianople, one can only wonder what Fritigern thought he could achieve by attacking the greatest fortress of the Empire. The Goths give the impression that they were wandering through the Eastern Empire without a map or a plan like something out of a 'yoof' package holiday. Retreating from the city, they spent the next few years destroying and looting in the Balkans.

The surviving Western Emperor, Gratian, elevated the Spanish general Theodosius first to *magister militum* and then to the purple on the 19th January, 379 AD. This was a most pivotal decision as the Theodosians were to preside over the destruction of the Western Empire. Theodosius was the son of a *comes*, a senior commander in the mobile army who had served in Britain and North Africa.

In 380 AD, the Gothic chieftains Alatheus and Saphrax attacked Pannomia and had to be bought off. Theodosius spent the next few years hunting down and deporting groups of barbarians 'holidaying' in the Balkans. In 382 AD, he accepted the inevitable and legalised Visigothic occupation of Imperial lands under their own chieftains. In return, the Visigoths undertook to provide allied troops as required. This was a feudal relationship. A dangerous new policy had been devised which would result in the dismemberment of the Western Empire. The first barbarian kingdom had been created within Imperial territory.

Around this time, a new and ambitious Persian king ascended the throne – Shapur III. Theodosius brokered a deal that turned much of independent Armenia into a Persian client state. Theodosius' policy of appeasement damped down the flames in the East, at least in the short term, but trouble was brewing in the West.

His own soldiers assassinated Gratian, the scholarly, un-military, emperor in 383 AD. They were angered by his preferential treatment of Alan mercenaries. The story is that the Emperor had taken to striding around dressed as a barbarian warrior. The *Comes Britanniarum*, Magnus Maximus, was probably behind the plot. He promptly revolted and Britain, Gaul and Spain declared for the rebel. North Africa and Italy remained loyal to the child emperor, Valentinian II,

On the march

under the control of his mother Justina. Theodosius, again following a policy of appeasement, recognised Maximus as Augustus, ie, a full emperor, and attacked Iuthungi, an Alamannic chief, in 384 AD.

Meanwhile, as the Roman generals squabbled, barbarian invasions continued. In 386 AD, a Gothic warlord called Greuthungi crossed the Danube to escape the Huns only to be killed in battle by the *magister peditum* Promotos. Many of his men survived to 'volunteer' for Theodosius' army.

In 387 AD, the unappeased Maximus advanced into Italy with Frank and Saxon allies to unseat Valentinian II. The young emperor and his mother fled to Theodosius for protection. His policy in tatters, the Eastern Emperor marched west with his barbarian allies and killed Maximus at the Battle of Aquileia in north-east Italy in 388 AD. Other detachments destroyed Maximus' troops in Africa and Sicily. Valentinian was appointed ruler of Gaul while Theodosius spent three years reorganising Italy. Then an astonishing event occurred, the fearsome Bishop of Milan, Ambrose, disagreed with Theodosius and forced the Emperor to publicly repent.

The Franks were not slow to exploit the latest Roman civil war and raided into Germania Secunda towards Cologne. The *magister militum* Arbogast, who was himself of Frankish descent, smashed the invaders in 389 AD devastating the territory of the Bructeri and Chamavi.

In 391 AD, Theodosius returned to Constantinople leaving the West to the hapless Valentinian II. Trouble was not long in coming. Valentinian became unhappy with his Frankish general and tried unsuccessfully to sack him. The quarrel was exacerbated by religion, as the Imperial family were Christian and the field marshal was a pagan. Arbogast mounted a coup, murdered the Emperor and installed the pagan rhetorician Eugenius on the Western throne. Another straw in the wind, barbarian-born generals were now making and unmaking puppet emperors. The weary Theodosius marched west once again in 394 AD and near Aquileia on the north-eastern border of Italy defeated the Western Roman army at the Battle of the Frigid River. A few months later he died. Arguably, the Empire died with him.

Theodosius has had a better treatment from history than perhaps he deserves. His title of 'The Great' refers more to his piety than his political skills. A reasonable general, he nevertheless seems to have lacked moral courage. Theodosius avoided conflict by mortgaging the future. His failure to deal with the Visigoths, his weakness before the Persians, his reluctance to replace inept members of the Imperial family by competent leaders, his tolerance of rebels, all created a spiral of decay in an age of crisis.

The will of Theodosius literally broke the Empire, dividing it between his young sons, Honorius and Arcadius. This poor military situation was exacerbated by massive losses at the great defeats in Persia and Adrianople. Added to this were the horrific casualties caused by rebellion and civil war. Finally, the wily Alaric with a Visigothic army at his back threatened the Empire from within. Romania now needed strong leadership to marshal its full resources to survive. It got division and the hopeless, hapless and helpless Theodosians.

THE EARLY FIFTH CENTURY

Puppet emperors had duly been appointed but the promotions that really mattered were the generalissimos behind the thrones. Theodosius' warlord Stilicho, descended from a Vandal soldier and married into the Imperial family, was marked down to lead the West. The problem was that the warlord claimed supremacy in the East as well, leading to endless conflict with Arcadius' advisors and hence between the Western and Eastern empires. After Theodosius, if the blame for disaster can be laid at anyone's door then it can be laid at Stilicho's. He continually duelled with Alaric but was unable, or unwilling, to destroy the Visigothic king. The duel sucked troops out of the West to Italy decreasing Western provincial security.

Disaster struck on the last day of the year in 406 AD. Massed hordes of barbarians, mostly Vandals, swept over the frozen Rhine. The Rhine limitanei disintegrated and were swept away like a child's sand castle on a beach hit by the first big wave of a rising tide. The tribesmen flowed across the north of Gaul and down the west coast inflicting considerable damage and dislocation. Stilicho failed to move to seal the breach. Britain rebelled in disgust, with Constantine being elevated to the purple. He then took the bulk of the British mobile army to Gaul, undoubtedly the correct strategic move but Britain itself was now largely undefended. It was not clear at that point but Romania had just lost Britain for all time.

Arcadius died on May 1st, 408 AD and his seven year old son Theodosius II was crowned. Stilicho saw this as his chance to get control of the Eastern throne. His solution in the West was to send Alaric as an ally to put down the usurper Constantine. This made some sense from the general's viewpoint but it sparked an anti-German rebellion amongst the citizens of the Western Empire. All the Romans could grasp was that Stilicho intended to use a dangerous barbarian warlord to destroy the last Roman army operating in the West.

'I cannot enumerate without horror all the calamities of our age. For the last twenty years and more, Roman blood has been shed daily between Constantinople and the Julian Alps. Scythia, Thrace, Macedonia, Dardania, Dacia, Thessaly, Achaea, Epirus, Dalmatia and both Pannonias have lain prey to Goths, Sarmatians, Quadi, Alans, Huns, Vandals and Macromans who have ravaged, destroyed and pillaged them.'

Eusebius Hieronymus (St. Jerome) c.342–420 AD

Negotiating with a warlord

recognised Constantine as an Augustus in 409 AD and then promptly changed his mind with masterly indecision. Constantine moved into Italy supposedly to assist Honorius against Alaric. Honorius received 4,000 reinforcements from Constantinople and Constantine retreated, suspicious that he rather than Alaric would be the target of Honorius' army.

The Vandal army crossed into Spain late in 409 AD and another province suffered destruction. In a mirror of earlier British reactions, the Spanish army rebelled at Constans' incompetence and appointed Maximus emperor. Maximus killed Constans and in 411 AD invaded Gaul and laid siege to Constantine in Arles. Honorius, meanwhile, had found a new *magister militum*, Constantius, who in 411 AD marched to Gaul with an army to restore the situation, ie, to fight with Roman rebels not barbarians. The Spanish army defected to Honorius, Maximus taking refuge with the barbarians in Spain. Arles was then captured. Constantine slipped off to a church for sanctuary and took priest's vows; he was still beheaded. Honorius' troops were winning the fight against their fellow Romans, but what of the barbarians?

Following Alaric's lead, the Burgundians and Alans in Mainz had appointed their own emperor, Jovinus. Alaric's successor, Ataulf, was appointed a Roman ally by Honorius to deal with Jovinus and his barbarian allies. Jovinus was duly beaten and his head joined the collection at Ravenna. The victorious Visigoths crossed into Gaul in 412 AD taking the pretender Attalus with them as a sort of mobile insurance policy. A '*keep your own spare emperor in the back of the wagon*' – no upwardly mobile barbarian chief should be without one!

Heraclian, the *comes*, who controlled the last unaffected province of North Africa, rebelled and invaded Italy. His army was carried in a fleet of reputedly 700 ships. Constantius crushed him by the Tiber and was rewarded with his estate. Supposedly one ship carried the remnants back across the Mediterranean. Another Roman army destroyed by Romans.

Roman civilisation slowly collapsed in Britain and in 410 AD Honorius instructed the inhabitants to arrange their own defence against the prowling Picts, Scots and Saxons. Many British migrated to Amorica under their leader Riothamus giving the region a new name, Brittany. This area became notorious for *bacaudae*.

Back in Gaul, the opportunistic Visigoths grabbed territory in the south. Ataulf married the Roman princess Galla Placidia. The legend is that Ataulf poured the treasure looted from Rome over the blushing bride. It was not long before Constantius was dispatched west to deal with the situation. The Visigoths migrated before his army to Barcellona in 414 AD following the Vandals but they left the pretender Attalus behind as a peace offering to Honorius. Ataulf died in Barcellona, murdered by Segericus who was promptly murdered a week later by Vallia. Barbarian politics tended to be somewhat robust, like the Mafia. When a leader was

The result was an anti-German backlash. Stilicho was executed and many barbarian soldiers in the army (reportedly 30,000) had to flee to the Visigoths for protection. Alaric marched into Italy devastating the rich peninsula and sacking Rome on the 24th August, 410 AD. Rome was not militarily important, it was not the capital of the Empire – that had been moved to Ravenna – it was not even a regional capital. But Rome was the spiritual centre of the Empire and the shock was immense. It had been 800 years since Rome had experienced the violence of a barbarian sacking.

The situation in the Western Empire was now strategically disastrous. The Rhine border was in flames, the limitanei there were withdrawn, fled or destroyed. A Vandal army ravaged northern and western Gaul causing immense damage. A Visigothic army devastated Italy and Britain was in rebellion. Honorius controlled few military assets of much consequence and the most effective Roman army in the west was under the control of a rebel. In the next few years, seven would-be-emperors fought each other for control of the West: Honorius, Attalus, Constantine, Constans, Maximus, Jovinus and Heraclion. The barbarians bled the Western Empire to death while its generals tussled over the corpse.

The key rebel, Constantine, crossed the channel to Boulogne and had some success against the barbarians, even shoring up the Rhine frontier for a while. The general pushed out forces loyal to Honorius and by 408 AD had control of Roman Gaul. Constantine promoted his son to Caesar and ordered him to Spain to take charge of the province. Honorius

deposed there was none of this '*spending more time with his family*' stuff.

Vallia, the new king, negotiated allied status with Honorius and as one of the clauses in the deal returned Galla Placidia. The lady was then married to Honorius' general Constantius who apparently had developed a severe lust for her. This lady was the ultimate trophy wife before trophy wives were invented. The Visigoths were given Aquitaine and in return hammered the Vandal army in Spain. Constantius died in 421 AD and the Emperor Honorius in 423 AD. Superficially, the Empire was restored; usurpers had been put down and barbarians chastised except for untouchable barbarians who were solemnly recognised as allies.

A closer look reveals terrible weaknesses. Britain was lost and Gaul, Spain and Italy had been devastated, severely reducing the Empire's tax yield. The Roman army had sustained massive losses, often in civil war. The Visigoths were a powerful independent state within the Empire. Also within imperial boundaries, parties of barbarians roved at will and the countryside in Gaul swarmed with *bacaudae*. Alarmingly, the Vandals had survived Visigothic attacks in southern Spain and in 422 AD defeated a Roman army sent to destroy them. They mastered naval technology, captured the Balearic Islands and raided North Africa. Franks moved into northern Gaul, sacking Trier in 419 AD. General Castinus was dispatched north to push back the future French but their leader Clodo seized territory as far south as the Somme. The next chapter of the history rotates around the astonishing career of the Lady Galla Placidia, sister and daughter of emperors and Queen of the Visigoths. After her return to Ravenna, Galla Placidia enjoyed such an intimate relationship with her half-brother Honorius that the social gossips were all a twitter. It could not last and the lady was soon on her way to exile in Constantinople after her Visigothic *bucellarii* clashed with the Emperor's troops. Upon the demise of Honorius, Theodosius II, the

eastern emperor, ruled Ravenna through Honorius' old general, Castinus. In 423 AD, Castinus rebelled and placed an administrator, *primicerius*, called John (Ioannes) on the Western throne. John received little support; his *Praetorian Prefect* in Gaul was promptly murdered. Galla Placidia recovered the throne for herself and her young son Valentinian III with the support of Constantinople, Carthage and the Visigoths. John lost his head, General Castinus fled and John's most dangerous supporter was bought off. He was a young man called Aetius who had great influence amongst the Huns. The Empress, as she now was, played off her two great generals, Aetius of Gaul and Boniface of North Africa. First one then the other had the Empress' favours until Aetius killed his rival.

Gaiseric, king of the Vandals, crossed the straits of Gibraltar in 429 AD and gradually took over North Africa, defeating Roman armies in the process. Carthage fell in 439 AD and another Roman province felt the lash of barbarian rule. The great buildings decayed where they were not deliberately destroyed. Gaiseric achieved official recognition as an 'ally' in 442 AD. Aetius was undisputed ruler of Gaul and in 436 AD, he used Hun allies to annihilate rebelling Burgundians while he fought the Visigoths.

THE LATE FIFTH CENTURY

A generation ended in 450 AD as Galla Placidia died leaving her son, Valentinian III, to make his own decisions – a task for which he was spectacularly ill equipped. In Constantinople Theodosius II died and was replaced by the energetic Marcian who cut off payments to the Huns, who were proving troublesome.

A Pictish ambush

Attila, the new king of the Huns, launched a huge army of barbarians against the Western Empire in 451 AD. Aetius built an unprecedented Gaulish confederation of Romans and Germans to oppose Attila, with himself as supreme warlord. The armies clashed on the Catalaunian Plains, the traditional site supposedly located near Chalons, and Aetius was triumphant.

Chalons was the most important battle of the late Western Empire. Aetius was fighting for the preservation of civilisation and the Germano-Latin cultures of France and southern Europe. Attila had very little to offer civilisation; a Hun attack left nothing but a depopulated and barren wasteland.

Attila survived with enough of his army to retreat back into the *Barbaricum* but in 452 AD invaded Italy. His army attacked with its customary ferocity, Aquileia was erased from the surface of the Earth. Aetius bided his time and moved his army into a blocking position to protect Gaul; his German allies would not leave their own territories. Marcian, the Eastern Emperor intervened by moving his army onto the Danube, across the rear of the Huns. The Hun army with its primitive logistics starved and was stricken with a terrible plague that had already ravaged Italy. The army retreated and within a year Attila was dead. He left the Hun Empire to his sons but in 454 AD the Ostrogoths rebelled and smashed it apart.

Aetius, whose fortunes had been so entwined with the Huns, also died in 454 AD, murdered by the jealous and pathetic Emperor. Valentinian was assassinated by two of Aetius' *bucellarii* in 455 AD. Petronius Maximus, a wealthy senator implicated in the killing of Valentinian, ascended the throne and married the late Emperor's widow. Valentinian's daughter, a seventeen year old princess called Eudocia, was married to Maximus' son. This marriage created a diplomatic incident as Eudocia had been promised at the age of five to Huneric, son of the Vandal warlord Gaiseric.

An outraged Gaiseric manned his fleet, sailed on Rome and sacked it thoroughly. Maximus tried to flee but was killed by the Roman mob. Gaiseric carried Valentinian's family in triumph back to Carthage and Huneric married Eudocia. It is not recorded what the princess thought of her love life. By now she was probably hoping to meet a frog!

Avitus, *magister militum* for Gaul, was the Visigoth's choice for Western Emperor and was duly recognised by Marcian. The Vandals raided Sicily in 456 AD and were defeated in a naval battle by another magister militum, the Visigoth Ricimer. This general deposed Avitus and put Majorian on the throne as Western Emperor in 457 AD. Majorian then made a show of strength in Gaul to confirm his authority. In Spain, Gaiseric destroyed a similar attempt and Ricimer executed the defeated Emperor. Once emperors executed defeated generals, now in the dying embers of the Empire the reverse occurred.

Ricimer made a nonentity called Libius Severus puppet emperor but events were moving against him as Carthage and Constantinople reached accord. So when Severus died in 465 AD, apparently of natural causes, Ricimer deferred to Emperor Leo and ruled the West as his agent. Gaiseric felt slighted and launched more raids, including the Eastern Empire amongst his targets. Leo took charge of events and appointed his own man, Athemius, as Western Emperor. A mighty expedition utilising the resources of both the Eastern and Western Empires was prepared to attack North Africa in 468 AD. Significantly, Ricimer was excluded. The expedition was a complete failure with disastrous results for what was left of the Western Empire.

The Visigothic king Euric gradually took over Roman territory until he controlled large chunks of Spain and southern Gaul, declaring independence in 475 AD. The Western Empire now consisted only of Italy and a patch of territory to the north. Ricimer killed Athemius in 472 AD and with Gaiseric's support clothed a new puppet, Olybrius, in purple. Both Ricimer and his puppet died of natural causes soon after.

A Burgundian called Gundobad, who was Ricimer's nephew, seized power and following a familiar pattern put a puppet, Glycerius, on the throne. Leo refused to recognise this arrangement and sent one of his own relatives, a general called Julius Nepos to rule. The new Emperor made Orestes, who had been secretary to Attila, his generalissimo and the latter repaid him by seizing power, hoping to rule through his son Romulus Augustulus.

But the German soldiers in Italy were through with puppet emperors. They wanted their own kingdom like the other barbarians and in 476 AD they elected as king Odovacer, a barbarian officer in the Roman army who had been a chieftain in Attila's army. He executed Orestes and in a show of mercy rare for the time deposed the young Emperor and sent him off to live in retirement on a pension in a castle by the Bay of Naples. Odovacer returned the Imperial Regalia to Constantinople and ruled as King of Italy.

The barbarian kingdoms were unable to maintain the road network, indeed, saw little need to do so. The Western Roman Empire was no more. The shining light of Roman civilisation was reduced to little flickers and the West slipped into the Dark Ages.

> '**B**ut when the appointed day came, Alaric armed his whole force for the attack and was holding them in readiness close by the Salarian Gate; for it happened that he had encamped there at the beginning of the siege. And all the youths at the time of the day agreed upon came to this gates and received Alaric and the army into the city at their leisure. And they set fire to the houses which were next to the gate, among which was also the house of Sallust, who in ancient times wrote the history of the Romans, and the greater part of this house has stood half-burned up to my time; and after plundering the whole city and killing most of the Romans, they moved on.'
>
> Alaric's Sack of Rome, 410 AD

·THE·ROMANS·

"We've killed thousands of Sarmatians, thousands of Franks again and again; we're looking for thousands of Persians."

Vita Aureliani

(We suspect this was an Auxiliary Palatine drinking song – Authors)

The Roman army was a professional force of servicemen whose essential experience of soldiering would be familiar to the men who followed Wellington, Montgomery or Stormin' Norman. The army employed between 300,000 to 600,000 men and was by far the biggest single organisation of the Roman state. We can distinguish three types of soldiers: *regulars, foederati, and allies.*

Foederati referred to barbarian units in the Roman army – as opposed to individual barbarians recruited as soldiers. In this period, foederati regiments appear to be units of a single type of barbarian, possibly recruited for a special skill, who were paid, equipped and treated as a regular Roman regiment. They were commanded by Roman officers and should be considered Roman regular army in the same sense that Gurkha regiments are regular British Army now. Cataphract cavalry may have originally been Sarmatian foederati. There are records of horse archer foederati being recruited from people like the Huns. Allies were a barbarian army fighting under its own leaders and using its own tactics but under Roman strategic command. In the 5th century, Roman armies commonly included significant numbers of allies.

As a rough guide, a Roman army consisted of two regiments of infantry for every regiment of cavalry. The only exception to this seems to have been elite *vexillationes palatini* which were 12:1 heavy to light cavalry. At the Battle of Strasbourg, Julian had 10,000 infantry and 3,000 cavalry. *Limitanei* may have had a higher proportion of cavalry to infantry because security duties required tactical mobility.

ROMAN STRATEGY AGAINST BARBARIANS

The Roman strategy against barbarians can be summed up as keeping them out at all costs and destroying them by any means if they penetrated Imperial boundaries. The most effective military way of achieving this was by 'perimeter defence', ie, concentrating the army at the border. In the early Empire this was the preferred strategy. In the later Empire, mobile armies were located deeper within Imperial territory.

This looks suspiciously to the modern eye like 'defence in depth' which is much admired these days by modern strategists. But ancient authors wrote approvingly of perimeter defence.

Perimeter defence has been the favourite defence of most nations throughout history. There are sound political and economic reasons not to fight a war on your own territory as implied by defence in depth. It is noteworthy that American planners in NATO were keen on defence in depth across continental Europe while the German and French governments were keener on perimeter defence. Would the Americans have been so keen on defence in depth if California was the planned battlefield?

Perimeter defence has had a pretty bad press in recent years for two reasons. First is the proven capacity of a mechanised army to concentrate, blast a hole in a perimeter defence and then speedily penetrate deep into the hinterland. The destruction of France by a handful of mobile Panzer divisions that bypassed the Maginot Line is the classic example of this. The second reason is that in the modern mechanised world, defending troops are so mobile on internal lines that they are best located centrally to be concentrated to meet an armoured thrust that may come from any direction.

However, neither of these reasons was, obviously, applicable to the Roman Empire. Barbarians were not fast moving armoured divisions and Roman mobile armies could not be quickly moved. They marched at infantry speed. The first mobile armies were under the personal control of the Emperor located wherever the Imperial Court was based at that time. The reason was probably political rather than military, the general with the biggest army could become Emperor whenever he wanted. Later, a compromise was found where a series of mobile armies were located closer to the borders.

The fastest speed that the Imperial post (*cursus publicus*) could deliver messages was 320km per day, although 80km was more normal. This limitation was critical in Imperial responses to barbarian raids.

Close combat

The garrison of a single fort could intercept a tiny raid. The concentrated forces of a single *dux* of *limitanei* would meet a larger raid. If a ducate was overwhelmed by an invasion, a centralised force would be created based on a regional mobile army possibly supplemented by limitanei units drawn from surrounding ducates. A major invasion would be opposed by a large force, with a praesental army as its core.

The mobile army might take weeks or even months to reach the threatened area. When it arrived, a number of events might occur. The first was a pitched battle. This was the favoured approach of Roman soldiery. With some justification, they had complete conviction in their status as highly trained, well-armed professionals and were keen to 'kick ass'. Their attitude was to get it all over with quickly, pick up their legitimate plunder and enjoy some well earned rest and recuperation among a grateful citizenry – and if they were not adequately grateful the flat of a *spatha* upon the rear would soon remind them of their social obligations.

Roman commanders were less keen on pitched battles knowing that once the gods started beating the war drums even the best laid plans could go wrong. Why risk all on a single roll of the dice! But the primary reason pitched battles were infrequent was that it needed the barbarians to co-operate. The barbarian chiefs were in this for plunder and status and there was little of either to be had when the *auxilia palatina* had finished putting one's warriors through a meat grinder. A battle was likely if the barbarians had concentrated for a siege or some other reason and the *regales* felt lucky. The Roman commander would be careful to engage only on favourable, ie, flat and open, terrain where the advantages of his troops would be most effective.

The preferred strategy of the Roman commanders at this time was to engage any dispersed barbarian raiders with attritional warfare through ambushes, hit and runs, and other sneaky

stratagems. The better intelligence, command control and troop quality of the Roman army was bound to prevail in small scale attritional warfare with no chance of losing half the army through some freak event.

If there were too many barbarians or if they were dispersed into dangerously difficult terrain which acted as a force multiplier for barbarian warriors, then the Romans would move into suitable blocking positions to contain the threat. Starving barbarians were prone to surrender. If the Roman commander was really fortunate, barbarians would attack his troops in their chosen defensive positions.

In extremis, the comitatenses would follow the barbarians into bad terrain to ambush them. One may be sure that this was only done where good intelligence was available.

Roman strategy was therefore largely reactive. The barbarians mostly had the initiative. If the Emperor (or some similarly high ranking personage) was present when news of trouble in the Barbaricum was received then he might decide to launch a pre-emptive strike, for example the Alamannic wars of Valentinian I, but this happened rarely and was mainly by chance. Mostly, the Roman mobile armies were in the position of a fire brigade or police force, rushing from crisis to crisis.

Where the Roman army invaded the Barbaricum the preferred strategy was a pincer movement on an objective from two jumping off points. If successful this could catch the barbarians between the two forces impeding their dispersion. The barbarian response was usually to disperse rather than risk a battle. There were, however, exceptions to this. In 357 AD, a pincer attack on the Alamanni failed when the barbarians engaged and defeated the southern arm commanded by Barbatio. If the barbarians fled, the Romans would plunder and destroy their crops and villages as a punitive measure '*pour encourager les autres*'. The purpose of this action was to force the canton leaders to formerly surrender and agree to discuss peace treaties. These tended to be adhered to by barbarian commanders who took any oaths they made seriously.

It is worth remembering that there were other, cheaper, ways to deal with barbarians than military action. Roman agents were constantly busy in the Barbaricum, involved in diplomacy, bribery and assassination. We mostly have the records of the diplomatic failures where combat became necessary.

ROMAN STRATEGY AGAINST REBELS

The Roman Empire had no accepted method of transferring power except by military force. By modern standards it was a military dictatorship. There was always the possibility that an ambitious, popular (popular with the soldiers – civilian opinion was irrelevant) general with a substantial army might reach for the purple. Generals might rebel from self-preservation; emperors were understandably paranoiac about successful, popular generals.

Unless a usurper could be assassinated, rebellion always resulted in civil war that continued until the Emperor or the usurper was dead. The strategy was therefore to engage an opponent's army on favourable terms and defeat it. As both sides would have equal capabilities victory commonly went to the biggest army.

The high morale in Roman armies and Roman combat techniques tended to mean that a decision was only reached when the defeated army was crushed and by then the winner had also taken heavy casualties. The losses in troops could be disastrous – 54,000 at Mursa. The situation was exacerbated by the execution of all the senior officers on the losing side.

Inevitably, civil war invited barbarian incursions. Feuding Romans often employed barbarian allies. This was dangerous but had the advantage of keeping barbarian forces occupied where one could keep an eye on them. Needless to say, barbarian allies were utterly untrustworthy.

Sieges were far more likely in civil wars than wars against barbarians. Who controlled which cities could be important in winning over neutral commanders. Civil war battles tended to occur at strategic choke points, eg, alpine passes. So naval lift capability was a significant advantage.

TACTICS

All strategic movement was carried out using the road network. March movement was carried out in columns (*agar quadratum*) proceeded by scouts. Cavalry took the point followed by the infantry. The baggage train followed the infantry or marched within their columns. An infantry unit followed and then cavalry formed the rearguard. In the vicinity of the enemy, an army moved into a broader formation with the infantry in columns and the cavalry on the wings. If necessary, the army split into three march columns.

A day's march covered 20km, the pack animals could not manage more than 30km. According to Bishop Ambrose they rested for one day in four. Fortified camps with a ditch and palisade were erected at the end of each day for sleeping and as a base camp in the presence of the enemy. Infantry would be left to hold the camp and the baggage train during battle.

The standard formation had the infantry drawn up in the centre in one or two lines with the cavalry on the wings. Heavy cavalry was deployed closest to the infantry, with light cavalry on the extreme flanks. A force of infantry and cavalry made up a reserve behind the line under the direct control of the general. Roman commanders were familiar with all the tricks: refused wings and centres, single envelopment and double envelopment.

SIEGES

The fortified site to be attacked was first blockaded to stop supplies and reinforcements getting in and the defenders getting out. Field fortifications were erected around the site. Essentially the blockaders then waited for the defender's food supply or nerve to fail. Blockades could go on for months or even years.

If the strategic situation warranted the cost in men, an assault could be mounted. This was often necessary in civil wars where strategic momentum was critical. The attacker's problem was to get his troops to the other side of the defender's curtain wall. The first step was to dominate the wall area by superior firepower, destroying the defender's

Lying in state

artillery and sweeping his troops from the parapets. This was possibly the role of the mobile artillery regiments. The defender's job was to prevent the attacker achieving such dominance. Artillery batteries were mounted on walls for this purpose.

Stone throwers (*scorpiones* and *onagri*) would be used for general bombardment while the more accurate bolt throwers (*ballistae*) could be aimed at specific targets. Archers, slingers and javelin throwers would add their firepower to the general storm. Fire arrows might be used to set light to the defender's buildings or the attacker's siege engines.

Assuming the attacker achieved firepower dominance in the wall region, the assault might begin. The ditch would be levelled so that siege engines could go up to the curtain wall. Siege towers and scaling ladders were often used to get men over defended walls. Sometimes earth mounds and ramps were constructed for the same purpose or rams and crowbars might be used to bring down the wall, or mines might be dug.

While this was going on the defenders would not be idle. They might hang various paddings on the walls to protect them. If part of the wall started to collapse, a new defensive wall might be built behind the damaged section. Attacks would be made on siege engines and countermining would be tried.

Once the defences were overcome the city would be stormed. By convention, its citizens could be massacred and the city sacked.

RECRUITS

The army needed 15,000 to 30,000 recruits (*tiro*) a year. Recruits were drawn from both volunteers and conscripts within the Empire. They were between 19 and 25 years old and normally served for between 20 to 24 years, probably in the same unit. Volunteers were likely to be drawn from the same sort of people who joined the colours in Napoleonic England – the adventurous, the desperate, or those who had made civilian life too hot to hold them.

Conscripts came from a variety of sources. The sons of soldiers were automatically conscripted. Many famous Roman soldiers were recruited in this way, eg, Silvanus, Stilicho and Asper. Annual levies were required from communities. This law was sometimes used to extort taxes. In the 5th century, supplemental levies were applied to certain classes, the *illustres* and *clarissimi*. Again, these could be commuted to a tax. Barbarian prisoners of war were fair game for conscription. This was a good deal, for both the barbarians and the Empire.

Recruits also came from outside the Empire. Substantial numbers of barbarians crossed the border to enlist in the ranks of Caesar's legions. Some of these were obtained as tribute but most were volunteers. We have no reliable way of working out exactly how many troops were of barbarian origin but Elton estimates it at a quarter. There is no evidence that barbarians were any less loyal to the army than internal recruits. Contrary to the text books, there is no evidence that recruitment from beyond Imperial borders reduced the effectiveness of the army any more than the Gurkha or Irish regiments wrecked the efficiency of the British Army. Soldiers of barbarian origin or descent could rise to the highest commands in the Roman army.

RANKS

A veteran soldier was called a *semissalis*. Private soldiers could be promoted through a series of NCO ranks: *circitor*, *biarchus*, *centenarius*, *ducenarius*, *senator*, and *primicerius*. There was a senior NCO grade called a *campidoctor*, which corresponds to drill sergeant or perhaps RSM. One of the veterans would be a standard bearer (*draconarius*) who carried the dragon standard, *draco*, which through the army of the Romano-British gave rise to the red dragon banner of Wales. Another veteran, the *bucinator*, was responsible for relaying orders by trumpet.

Units also had chaplains and doctors (*medicus*) on their strength.

LIMITANEI

Limitanei is a general term for the non-mobile army that guarded the borders. Other names used in the literature include *castellani*, *ripenses*, *riparienses and burgarii*. Whether these titles indicated meaningful differences in function is unclear. Limitanei were static in the sense that their units were not moved strategically. Tactically they marched at the same speed as the field army. Their units are described by a bewildering array of titles, some traditional, others 'modern'. There were also cavalry *alae* and *equites* and infantry *legiones*, *cohortes*, *limites*, *milites*, *auxilia*, *gentes* and *numeri*.

It is uncertain whether these titles indicated anything other than historical traditions. The modern British Army has a love of traditional regimental titles (dragoons, light infantry, lancers, grenadiers, yeomanry, riflemen, and guards) which mean little.

The functions of the border troops included policing, intelligence and raid interception. Policing involved stopping Roman deserters escaping and preventing the export of banned goods (eg, gold or weapons – 'gun-runners' were a problem). The combat power of limitanei is difficult to assess, as, inevitably, we tend to hear only of their failures in the records. Only raids in excess of 400 warriors are described in the records so we may assume that smaller raids were dealt with locally.

It seems likely that limitanei units were quite small; possibly 600 or less for infantry units and half that for cavalry. Legiones were often subdivided into up to half a dozen units. If these legiones were the same size as mobile legiones then their subunits would have been small indeed (approximately 200 men) so the suggestion has been made that border legiones were bigger at about 3,000 soldiers, giving subunits of 500 men.

Limitanei units were commanded by *tribuni* (if cohortes), *praefecti* (if legiones or their detachments), or *praepositi* (the other units). A general in charge of a number of units in a region was called a *dux* (Duke). For example, the general who commanded the troops on Hadrian's Wall had the title of Dux Britanniarum. Eight limitanei commands were called *comes* as in *Comes Litoris Saxonici* – the Count of the Saxon Shore, whose men manned the forts that can still be seen along the south-eastern coastline of Britain. There were twelve limitanei commands along the Rhine-Danube frontier.

A *limitanei dux* or *comes* was under the command of the regional *magister militum*.

Fleets or *classes*, were sometimes attached to limitanei forts. These are described as light, shallow draught boats (*lusoriae*) of more than one design, proportioned about 10m by 4m. They were primarily transports, carrying 300 men, but some probably mounted light artillery.

COMITATENSES

The *comitatenses* were grouped into a number of mobile armies. Each commander of Imperial rank (there was usually more than one) had a praesental force of comitatenses, including *scholae*. The Western praesental army was normally based in Italy when not on campaign. Other comitatenses were grouped into the regional mobile armies based deep within the Empire. Regional armies were fluid, being created and decommissioned as the situation demanded. Units and brigades were moved between armies as necessary.

Regional armies varied in size. There were an estimated 113,000 comitatenses in the West and 104,000 in the East. If correct, this would make the total Gaulic army in excess of 30,000 men but Julian commanded only 13,000 men in Gaul.

The mobile army was divided into cavalry *vexillationes* of perhaps 300 to 600 horse and infantry units of *legiones* of 1,200 foot and *auxilia* of 600 (or perhaps 1,200). It is likely that regiments were rarely at full strength. Mobile regiments are also referred to as *numeri*. 'Mobile' indicates that these units lacked a fixed station and could be moved strategically. It does not have the modern meaning of fast moving forces.

A *tribune*, or *praepositus* commanded units. Regiments often seem to have been permanently organised into brigades of two regiments commanded by a *comes* (count). For example, the elite Palatina Auxilia Celtae and Petulantes formed a brigade, as did the Heruli and Batavi. *Comes* was also the title for a general commanding a regional mobile army. For example, the commander of the British mobile army was titled the Comes Britanniae.

The leaders of the army were called *magister*, field marshal or general. Exact titles varied through time. In 400 AD, in the West there were two field marshals of equal status called *magister equitum* (literally master of the horse) and *magister peditum* (literally master of the foot). If the Emperor was weak, there were endless political manoeuvrings between the two. A dominant magister rapidly became a generalissimo. Arbogast was one of the first, but by no means the last. The Roman army seems to have been admirably free of racial barriers in this era as barbarian-descended officers could become magisters.

In the East, there were five *Magister Utriusque Militiae* (literally master of both branches of the army). Usually two commanded mobile armies directly under the Emperor's control (ie, praesental) while the others commanded the mobile armies of the Dioceses of Thrace, Illyricum and the Orient. Ferrill points out that the magisters of the East were less powerful than the West. This meant that the Eastern army was more dependent on an Emperor's personal leadership than the Western but on the other hand there was less chance of over-mighty generalissimos developing.

'But when the barbarians, rushing on with their enormous host, beat down our horses and men, and left no spot to which our ranks could fall back to deploy, while they were so closely packed that it was impossible to escape by forcing a way through them, our men at last began to despise death, and again took to their swords and slew all they encountered, while with mutual blows of battle-axes, helmets and breastplates were dashed in pieces. Then you might see the barbarian towering in his fierceness, hissing or shouting, fall with his legs pierced through, or his right hand cut off, sword and all, or his side transfixed, and still, in the last gasp of life, casting round him defiant glances. The plain was covered with carcasses, strewing the mutual ruin of the combatants; while the groans of the dying, or of men fearfully wounded, were intense, and caused great dismay all around.'

Ammianus Marcellinus,
The Battle of Hadrianopolis, 378 AD

As in the east, Western magisters could be attached to Dioceses. For example, the Magister Equitum Intra Gallas was the commander of the Gaulic army in the early 5th century. Eventually, a marshal came to be called just a *magister militum*. In the 5th century, the senior Western general was given the rank *Patricius*. The greatest generals of the Western Empire held this title (or equivalent); examples include Stilicho, Constantius, Boniface, Aetius, Ricimer and Odovacer.

The mobile army had a defined seniority: *Scholae*, *Palatina*, *Comitatenses* then *Pseudocomitatenses*. Cavalry outranked infantry, which is ironic as it tended to be the cavalry that let the army down in the great battles. Some units were split into *Seniores* and *Iuniores*, the former outranked the latter. *Clibanarii* were senior to *cataphractarii*. Old units outranked newly formed units. What effect all this ranking had in practice is unclear.

Scholae were all cavalry units of about 500 horses. They were the elite Imperial Guards and would normally take the field with a commander of Imperial rank (praesental). There were five regiments in the West and seven in the East. *Palatina* were originally praesental but in this era were crack field troops. There are some interesting references to Auxilia Palatina in *Ammianus Marcellinus*. As well as standing in the line of battle they seem to have been used as assault commandos discarding their armour and heavy weapons. This example is from Julian's campaign on the Rhine in 357 AD.

'Julian learning from some scouts… the river (Rhine) was fordable, encouraged a body of light armed auxiliaries under Bainobaudes, the tribune of the Cornuti… Wading through the shallows and at times supporting themselves on their shields and swimming, they reached a nearby island, where they landed and slaughtered everyone they found like sheep, without distinction of age or sex. Then, finding some empty boats, they went on in them, rickety though they were, and forced their way through a number of similar places. Finally, when they were sick of slaughter, they all returned safe with a rich haul of loot…'

Another example of the 'gung ho' attitude of the Palatina comes from the Siege of Amida in 359 AD by the Persians. The 'Gauls' were enraged at seeing Persian ill treatment of captured elderly Roman citizens. They resolved to assassinate the king in a night-sally by cutting their way through the numerically superior, professional Persian army. Ammianus Marcellinus, an eyewitness, takes up the story:

'Meanwhile the Gauls, refusing to wait any longer, emerged from a postern gate armed with axes and swords, taking advantage of a dark night… then in close order they made a furious charge, killed some of the pickets, and cut down the sentries… the groans of the dying roused many of the enemy… hordes of furious Persians… were flocking to the fight from every side. The Gauls stood their ground with unshaken strength and courage as long as they could, hacking at the enemy with their swords, but when some of their number had fallen or been wounded by the hail of arrows which rained on them, and they realised that the converging battalions of the foe were concentrating their whole weight on a single spot, they made haste to withdraw. None of them, however, turned his back and when they could no longer sustain the pressure… allowed themselves to be gradually pushed outside the rampart… these tactics allowed the Gauls to enter (Amida) about daybreak… their total losses that night amounted to 400 men.'

Possibly not the most sophisticated siege strategy, but there was clearly nothing wrong with the fighting spirit and battle craft of the mobile army.

Pseudocomitatenses were simply *limitanei* co-opted into the mobile army.

THE POOR BLOODY INFANTRY

Most infantry (*pedes*) fought in close order in the battle line. Perhaps a quarter to a third of an infantry regiment would be trained as bowmen. Ammianus gives an interesting anecdote taken from Procopius' revolt in 365 AD. The usurper stopped a battle between two auxilia palatina and a legion by rushing between the sides when '*they were exchanging missilia*'. As Elton points out, *missilia* must mean arrows as hand thrown weapons were discharged at close range. The implication is that Roman infantry regiments were mixed units capable of laying down considerable firepower before impact. As most barbarians wore no armour, this was a viable tactic. Some units seem to have been composed solely of archers (*sagittarii*).

A number of regiments had names that might indicate special roles, eg, *lancearii* or *exploratores*. But it is likely that these were of historical importance and did not reflect current practice. Seven regiments of balistarii (presumably artillery) are listed in the *Notitia Dignitatum*. Three were *legiones comitatenses*, three *pseudocomitatenses*, and one *limitanei*. It is not clear whether these artillery regiments ever fought in the field, as opposed to sieges.

THE CAVALRY

A cavalryman was called an *eques*. *Scutarii*, *promoti*, *armigeri*, *brachiati*, *cornuti*, *stablesiani*, etc, shock cavalry, made up two thirds of comitatenses cavalry regiments. Around fifteen per cent were cataphractii or clibanarii, heavily armoured shock cavalry (or some maybe had bows). Heavy armoured cavalry were stationed mainly in the east. The rest, including *equites sagittarii*, *equites mauri* (from Illyricum), *equites cetrati* and *equites dalmatae* were light cavalry. All except the first, who were bowmen, probably carried javelins. The Western scholae consisted of five shock regiments, the Eastern scholae of five shock units, one clibanarius and one sagittarius.

EQUIPMENT

Roman infantry used a variety of missile weapons. The primary long range missile weapon was the composite bow, used by both infantry and cavalry. It is possible that bowmen were concentrated in special units rather than mixed in with shock troops – the unit names seem to suggest this. Crossbows (*manuballistae*) existed but there is little evidence that they were used in battle. Slings (*fundi*), and staff slings (*fustibuli*, a sling on the end of a wooden staff) do not seem to have been commonly used in field battles. Slings were employed in sieges and may have been the weapon of choice for irregulars. Stones were thrown from the ramparts in sieges.

Short range missile weapons included heavy darts (*plumbatae* and *martiobarbuli*) which infantrymen carried in the hollow of their shields, and a variety of javelins (*spicula*, *verruta*, *hastae*, *pila*, *iacula* and *tela*). They seem to have been different weights, for example a *spiculum* was a 1.65m heavy armour piercing weapon while a *verrutum* was a 1m light javelin.

The standard infantry and cavalry hand-to-hand weapon was a thrusting/throwing spear (*lancea*) about 2m-2.5m long. Cavalry used an underarm one, or two-handed thrust as well as the overarm strike despite not having stirrups (the value of stirrups has often been exaggerated). Troops also carried a long, straight two-edged pointed sword called a *spatha* that could be used for cutting or thrusting. It was about 0.7m-0.9m long.

All troops wore metal helmets. There were two main types but the significance of this, if any, is unclear. The early type was the *spangenhelm*. This consisted of six (commonly) segments that fitted together like orange segments with the crown of the helmet as the pole. Reinforcing plates covered the joins. The second, later type was the 'ridge helmet' consisting of two halves joined together by a central dorso-ventral ridge. Helmets had neck and cheek guards attached at the rear and sides, and a nose guard on the front.

Both cavalry and infantry were clad in metal armour. Mail was the most common type but scale corselets were also known. Mail armour was made of iron while scales would be commonly bronze, which was brass coloured in the Roman world. Officers sported a bronze or iron cuirass. Sometimes leather pteruges were attached to the skirt and sleeves.

Troops usually carried large oval shields, 1m-1.2m high and 0.8m wide. Round shields also existed but seem to be mostly associated with the Emperor's immediate associates. Each unit had distinctive coloured patterns on its shield. These served the purpose of regimental colours.

As well as weapons and armour, soldiers were required to carry 20 days worth of rations, a blanket, tent quarter, stake, water bottle and pickaxe. Soldiers wore boots, a woollen tunic, trousers and a military cloak (*chlamys*) – possibly 25 kg-30 kg of kit in all.

At the start of this period, troops were issued with clothes so units would exhibit a degree of uniformity, however, by the 5th century soldiers were often issued with an allowance and bought their own clothes. This would tend to give a heterogeneous appearance particularly in the mobile army.

> '*D*ay had hardly dawned when the trumpets on both sides gave the signal for battle. The barbarians, after taking their customary oath to stand by one another, attempted to reach some hilly ground from which they could rush down as if on wheels and carry all before them by the impetus of their attack. In view of this our men hurried to their stations and stood fast; no one strayed or left the ranks to make a sally. When both sides had advanced cautiously and halted, the opposing warriors glared at each other with mutual ferocity. The Romans raised their morale by striking up a battle-cry; this begins on a low note and swells to a loud roar, and goes by the native name of 'barritus'. But the barbarians roared out rude chants in praise of their forefathers, and, while this discordant clamour in divers tongues was going on, skirmishing began. After an exchange of javelins and other missiles at long range, the opposing sides clashed and fought foot to foot with their shields locked in tortoise formation.'
>
> Ammianus Marcellinus

Soldiers' clothes were similar to civilian wear. An undyed or bleached tunic would be coloured anything from white to British Leyland beige. Or the tunic could be dyed green, yellow, blue or red. The latter seems suitably military. A variety of leg coverings were worn, trousers, breeches or puttees. Brown would be common or red-brown. The cloak might be in autumn colours, red-brown or yellow-brown.

Roman army equipment, especially weapons, was manufactured in thirty five state armouries called *fabricae*. We know of their existence from the Notitia but none have been identified archaeologically. Each frontier diocese had two fabricae while each frontier province boasted a *fabrica scutaria*. Some factories specialised in specific equipment such as weapons, artillery, cataphract armour, etc. They were positioned back from the front in safe areas on major road networks, presumably within fortified cities or forts.

BATTLE

Before battle Roman soldiers ideally had a good night's sleep in a safe fortified camp and just before dawn, trumpets woke them for breakfast. The Roman army was firmly of the opinion that an army fought on its stomach. After their meal, the soldiers paraded in full battle gear for inspection. At this point orders were given, the battle situation outlined and rousing speeches made.

The units marched out of the camp in a battle column, a simple right-angled turn to the left or right of the army standard bringing them into the battle line. Eventually, the infantry in the line closed with the enemy, and/or visa versa. At about 250m the lines were within bow range. Roman sagittarii opened fire either as units or as a single or double line drawn up behind the shock infantry, shooting over their heads. This fire was harassing rather than decisive but it prevented a barbarian unit halting for long when within bow range. Barbarians, at this time, had few bowmen and could not reply effectively.

At this point the opposing sides attempted to terrify their foes with a war cry – the *barritus*. At 50m both sides released a hail of close range missiles. Then units started to take significant casualties. Assuming neither side fled, one or both sides charged into hand-to-hand combat with spears and swords. Missiles continued to be exchanged by the rear ranks. A rugby scrum then ensued with some individuals taking weapon wounds or slipping and being trampled.

At some point one side started to lose ground or morale broke for some reason. Men then ran from the rear ranks and eventually the formation disintegrated. The losing side took serious casualties as men tried to disengage and flee.

The first target of the cavalry was the opposing cavalry. A cavalry engagement was a series of swift skirmishes as squadrons charged, wheeled and reorganised to charge again. If one side broke it would be pursued, taking casualties as it fled. The flank of the enemy infantry line would then be exposed. Cavalry were at a severe disadvantage if they attacked formed infantry from the front. But if they could work their way round the flank or rear of an engaged infantry line they could wreak havoc. Cavalry were also important in pursuing fleeing infantry, inflicting terrible casualties and preventing the panicked soldiers from reforming.

> "**A** deserter from the Scutari informed them that Julian was left with only 13,000 men. The distance from the Romans' starting point to the barbarians' entrenchment was 21 miles.
>
> A standard bearer suddenly shouted 'Follow Caesar, the guidance of your lucky star. You are fortune's darling, and in you we see that valour and judgement are at last combined'. These words put an end to all delay; the army moved forward.
>
> The Germans had been crossing the river (Rhine) for three days and nights. When our commanders saw them a short way off, forming themselves into dense wedges, they halted. The (Roman) vanguard with their standard bearers and junior officers made as if it were an impregnable wall, and the enemy showed like caution and stood still in their formations, they saw all our cavalry drawn up on our right flank, they massed all their strongest mounted men on their own left flank, interspersed with light-armed infantry.
>
> All these warlike and savage tribes were led by Chnodomarius and Serapio, whose power exceeded that of the other kings. Chnodomarius rode with a flame coloured plume on his head before the left wing. The right wing was led by Serapio, a young man. These two were followed by the next most powerful kings, five in number, by ten princes and a long train of nobles, and an army of 35,000 men.
>
> Severus, who commanded the Roman left wing, came in his advance near (hidden) troops. Severus halted suspecting an ambush. The Caesar had an escort of 200 horsemen.
>
> When the traditional signal to engage was sounded on both sides, a violent battle ensued. After a short exchange of missiles the Germans rushed forward brandishing their weapons and throwing themselves upon our cavalry. While our left wing, moving in close order, had thrown back the columns of Germans... our cavalry on the right unexpectedly gave way in disorder... The Caesar, seeing from a distance his cavalry turning to flight, put spurs to his horse and threw himself in their path.
>
> Then the Alamanni, having defeated and scattered our cavalry, attacked the front line of our infantry... they burst upon our line and forced their way as far as the legion of Primani, which was stationed at the centre of our position, in the formation known as the 'Praetorian camp'. Here the troops were drawn up in close formation in several ranks... at last they (the Germans) gave way under the stress of disaster and put all their efforts into attempts at flight.
>
> The Romans had lost 243 men and four officers. Of the Alamanni, however, 6,000 bodies were counted."
>
> Marcellinus

BUCELLARII

It was normal for Roman generals during this era to have a private bodyguard of 200 to 300 elite warriors, just like barbarian warlords. Originally, they were Roman regulars but by the 5th century they could have been of any type of soldier, mercenaries, foederatii or allies and were normally mounted. Barbarians made excellent bucellarii because they took personal oaths of allegiance to a leader very seriously. Bucellarii were supposedly named after *bucellatum*, a dried biscuit or hard tack found in army rations.

ARCANI

These were secret agents based on the borders that scouted and obtained intelligence in the Barbaricum for the army. They may have reported directly to the Emperor through the office of the magister officiorum. Ammianus Marcellinus describes the British arcani role as to *'hurry around here and there over long distances and give news of trouble among neighbouring peoples to our military leaders'*. Only the British agents are mentioned in the account but we may surmise that similar intelligence specialists were used along the Rhine and Danube. No doubt they also carried out 'special assignments' such as assassination.

In 370 AD, for example, Valentinian was reported as exchanging intelligence with the *regales* of the Burgundians through the agency of *'certain quiet loyal men'*. These 'quiet' men appeared to have killed a barbarian called Vithicabius.

BACAUDAE

The social system began to collapse in the Western Empire's death agony. Grinding tax hikes wiped out the middle classes, including small farmers whose holdings were taken over by ever richer big landowners. Many of the impoverished took to the hills and became bandits, *bacaudae*. Eventually, they became so powerful that they formed rebel armies and states, minting their own coins. They had the power to storm and plunder cities and control whole areas. Controlling the bacaudae became one of the primary duties of Roman 5th century warlords, such as Aetius. The placement of allied barbarian forces within the Empire was often conditioned by the need to hold down bacaudae. These rebels were mostly found in large numbers in the Western Dioceses in Britain, Spain and Gaul.

MILITIA

Roman administration did not encourage the formation, arming or training of a civilian militia except in extreme circumstances. So militia were always ad hoc Dad's Army affairs. When Roman ambassadors told Alaric in 408 AD that the inhabitants of the city had formed a militia, the deeply unimpressed warlord remarked that *'thick grass was easier to mow than thin'*.

PROTECTORES AND DOMESTICI

Nominally regiments commanded by the *comes domesticorum*, the *protectores* and *domestici* were not combat units but served as staff colleges for young officers. Members served as security officers and staff officers attached to a *magister militum*. After a suitable period of about five years they were promoted to unit commanders as *tribuni* or *praefecti*.

Eventually, the system fell into disfavour and these regiments became ornamental, as a sort of honorary position in the palace.

FORTIFICATIONS

Fortification of strategic points or resources was a common and effective military tactic of the late Empire. Forts served a number of functions. Correctly positioned, they acted as observation points and provided safe custom posts to impede the movement of deserters, both enemy and Roman. They also provided a secure jumping off point for raids and patrols into enemy territory. Great care was taken to locate forts where they controlled lines of communication. Forts came in a variety of sizes from *limitanei* garrison headquarters to tiny watchtowers (*burgi* or *terres*). They were largely built in the border zones, sometimes in the Barbaricum as well as Romania.

Roman forts were the predecessors of medieval castles. They were surrounded by one, or more, rings of ditches (*fossa*). These prevented siege engines and devices being brought up to the wall without prior preparation. Also, attackers scrambling out of the ditch were vulnerable to missiles as they could not maintain a shield wall. There is no evidence that ditches were filled with water but obstacles such as pit traps, stakes or caltrops (*tribuli*) were certainly employed to impede movement.

The main defence was a curtain wall made of stone, sometimes with a rubble core, about 1.5m-3m thick. The rampart walk level was 9m high and troops on it were protected by a crenellated parapet. Corner towers projected out to give enfilading fire positions and similar intervaled towers were placed along walls of any length at about 30m intervals. No fort towers have survived intact but they were probably about 15m-20m high. Artillery engines were probably sited on the towers.

Small forts had one gate, larger forts had two, flanked by towers. Portcullises were often used and the wooden gates were sheathed in iron for added protection. The inside of a fort would contain timber buildings built against the curtain walls.

Forts could be supplemented by linear defences along the borders. These were built in much the same way. The most famous are the walls that cut off peninsulas, eg, Hadrian's Wall in Northern England or the Long Walls at Constantinople. But defensive lines were erected to control mountain passes or river valleys.

Cities and towns in threatened areas, eg, most of Britain, were also fortified by defences rather similar to a fort. The walls rarely enclosed more than 10 hectares often leaving many buildings outside the protected area. The area inside the walls was known as the *urbs* or *oppidum* while buildings outside were part of the *civitas* or *suburbanus*. It must be stressed that fortifications were useless without a garrison and that artillery acted as a force multiplier rather than a defence in itself.

As Imperial defences collapsed, the fortified areas of cities shrank and Celtic hill forts were refortified as refuges for the rural population, eg, at South Cadbury. Similarly, villas were fortified as banditry increased.

NAVY

The late Roman navy seems to have been under the control of the army and contained both transports and fighting galleys that had rams. The larger warships would have carried an army's artillery. The main function of the navy was intercepting sea raiders and escorting transport fleets. Specially designed transports were created that carried cavalry units.

The fleet had a normal lift capacity of 5,000 men. For example, in 398 AD, 5,000 men were transported from Italy to Africa. Similar sized armies were taken to Britain in 360 AD and 367 AD. Constantinople lifted a full 8,000 men to Italy in 508 AD.

The standard warship design was the *dromon*, which means racer. Dromons were light cataphract (ie, enclosed) galleys with one bank of oars. They were about 15m long, had twenty two oars and displaced 17 tons displacement with a crew of 35.

Foederati

·THE·BARBARIANS·

"Above all it must be recognised that wild nations are pressing upon the Roman Empire and howling about it everywhere, and treacherous barbarians, covered by natural positions, are assailing every frontier."

Anonymous author of De Rebus Bellicis.

INTRODUCTION

There has been a tendency in wargaming circles to treat various groups of barbarians as if they were different nations with noticeably variant military structures or weapons. This is probably misleading as archaeological evidence suggests that barbarian society was the same everywhere except for broad constraints forced by geography, terrain and ecology. Many names for different barbarian groupings have come down to us. For example, the Attacotti are mentioned three times in Roman literature in the context of a threat to Britain. Who they were and where they lived is a complete mystery but is probably of little consequence as they would have been just like all the other Western barbarians.

The Romans classed barbarians into broad groups that can be further lumped together by language. The first were the Celtics. The Scotti lived in Ireland and were a threat to Britain as sea raiders. The Picts came from Scotland and again were mostly a maritime threat to Britain although they did share a land border. The next group were the Germans. Saxons occupied the marshy territory north of the Rhine on the North Sea coast. The two main Rhine confederations were the Francs in the north (lower Rhine) and the Alamanni in the south (upper Rhine). East of the Alamanni were the Burgundians. On the Western Danube lived the Quadi. The Sarmatians, who were related to the Persians, were to the east. North of these groups were the Vandals. Further east in the Danubian Basin were the Goths and the Alans. North-east lay the steppes, from whence came the Huns. Alans and Huns spoke a non Indu-European language and are usually thought of as Asiatic rather than European.

These assorted barbarians can be divided functionally into broadly three types. In the west, they were sedentary subsistence farmers. They grew a variety of cereals and vegetables and kept pigs, cattle and sheep. East of the Danube's bend on the Hungarian plains, the land was less suited to agriculture and the people were semi-sedentary. Hunting, fishing and animal herding had a more important role in their economies. Horse herding would not be uncommon. This was the lifestyle of the Goths and Sarmatians. Further east on the steppes were the true nomadic pastoralists, the Alans and the Huns. They herded sheep and cattle, moving from pasture to pasture in wagons. Horses were very important to such societies. As a barbarian group moved west its economy, and hence military capability, changed to match the ecology of the area. Current geographic location dictated barbarian army types more than racial or cultural origins.

> 'In every battle it is not numbers and untaught bravery so much as skill and training that generally produce the victory.'
>
> Vegetius

ORGANISATION

Barbarian society was non-urban and illiterate. The people lived in villages or groups of hamlets dominated by wealthy families called *optimates* by the Romans. Optimates were not necessarily tied to one place; they might have, for example, followed a successful warlord. A number of these social units formed a *pagus* or canton, ruled by a regales or minor king. The important quality of regales was their ability to lead the optimates and warriors into battle, rather than their royal blood or even kinship links. Regales would have had their own armed retinue of elite warriors known as *comitatus* (or *bucellarii*) who were the nearest thing barbarian leaders had to professional soldiers.

The Alamannic army at the Battle of Strasbourg, 357 AD, illustrates how this works. Two warlords, Chnodomarius and Serapio with 200 comitatus each, led five regales of various ranks and 35,000 warriors. Five cantons were involved but there were additional mercenaries and 'volunteers' in the army. Large armies were held together by the personal prestige and power (*potestate*) of successful warlords. There was little in the way of a national or tribal structure.

MILITARY OPERATIONS

Barbarians were likely to mount two forms of military operation: the raid and land acquisition. In barbarian society, a leader held potestate by virtue of leading his men in war and taking booty, which could then be distributed amongst his followers as gifts. Gift giving was the glue that bound warrior societies together. The Roman Empire was a natural target for such activity because it was rich.

Barbarian raids were a product of barbarian culture and should not be interpreted as a sign that barbarian leaders hated or intended to destroy the Empire. A statistical analysis by Elton demonstrated that raids came in waves, probably because if one barbarian leader mounted a raid then others would have to do likewise or lose face. Occasionally, raids were mounted in reprisal for Roman activity, itself probably a reprisal for barbarian incursions. The scenario is reminiscent of the situation the British Empire faced on the north-west frontier.

The most valued loot was treasure, precious metals and jewels, as they were valuable and portable. Roman military equipment was also desirable and food was welcome. Plunderers would mount cattle raids, driving animals before them at a maximum of 30 km per day. Raiding forces moved quickly on the outlap but could get bogged down on the run home. Human captives for ransom or slaves were another favourite and this was how the Romano-British St Patrick came to Ireland. Most raids occurred close to the border to get the spoils home but sea raids could go much further.

Most raids were fairly small scale affairs involving warriors from a single canton and probably had a maximum of 2,000 men. A more common size would probably have been 200 *effectives*. Just occasionally, a mighty warlord of high prestige might stitch together a great raid of up to 40,000 warriors. These could be truly dangerous to outnumbered Roman armies.

Marine raids are less well documented but apparently not uncommon. One recorded raid in 455 AD involved seven ships (400 men) of Heruli from the mouth of the Rhine to the coast of Spain. Barbarians had no naval combat capability, the boats probably resembled Viking longships (although the presence of masts is disputed). It seems possible that small numbers of horses could be carried but it is likely that sea raiders were infantry.

The larger the raid, the more quickly it would break down into smaller groups searching for food. Barbarian forces had little to no logistical capability. Their tactic was to move dispersed and only concentrate when threatened by the approach of a Roman force. This was to have unexpected consequences at the Battle of Adrianople.

The second type of barbarian military operation was armed migration with the intention of settling on new lands. Ideally, the barbarians would peacefully move into Imperial territory, with or without Imperial permission, but they were prepared to fight their way in if necessary. Roman weakness could invite migrations but often such movements were the result of desperate people avoiding a more fearsome barbaric foe, such as the Huns. A migrating group would have to move more slowly than a raid as it was burdened by wagons. A rough guide is that a quarter or less of a population of barbarians would be warriors.

The Huns

TACTICS

The primary barbarian tactic was to avoid getting into an open pitched battle with Roman forces since they were almost certain to get hammered. Even superior numbers did not always help, as the Romans were quite capable of winning at a 3:1 disadvantage. Bad terrain, which disrupted Roman formations and command control, and impeded long range missile fire was a definite plus, all the more so if the Romans could be persuaded to walk into an ambush. Even in a full scale pitched battle, barbarian leaders attempted to utilise terrain to spring ambushes. Roman commanders were wise to this tactic, eg, Strasbourg.

Barbarian infantry formed up into a line of deep attack columns called *cunei* (wedges or swine's head formations). The ancient writer Vegetius describes a *cuneus* as a triangular formation, which makes no tactical sense. Tacitus describes it more as a close formation, deep attack column and this is entirely believable as a formation designed to break enemy lines in hand-to-hand combat. When the cuneus advanced into combat, it is likely that the warriors in the centre, being most protected, surged forward, while those on the flanks tended to hang back, resulting in a convex frontage and hence 'wedge'. It is probable that each barbarian cuneus represented a kinship group, probably from a single canton. In attack, the Germans bolstered their morale with the barritus, the war cry. The warriors held their shields in front of their mouths as amplifiers and built up a hard staccato roar of increasing crescendo.

Skirmishing missile troops throwing javelins, spears or axes might have been used to protect the front of the cunei. The ideal was to cross through the superior Roman fire power zone as fast as possible, charging while raising the barritus. The wild charge of the attack columns had to carry the Roman units away, as the barbarians were unlikely to win a long melee. The flanks were protected by skirmishers or cavalry.

Sack of Rome

Shock attack cavalry were the finest troops in most barbarian armies and would be used to deliver the critical blow. Eastern armies would field cavalry using classic light tactics of hit and run, releasing a shower of missile weapons. Infantry might be drawn up into two lines but it is doubtful whether barbarian command control ran to reserves.

The ratio of cavalry to infantry in a barbarian army was probably about 1:5 in Western armies rising to 1:3 in Eastern armies. Barbarian armies from settlements within the Empire might field an army of one quarter to one third cavalry.

SIEGE CAPABILITY

Generally, the siege capability of barbarian armies can be summarised as non-existent. Barbarians could blockade walled towns but commonly they ran out of food before the defenders because of their poor logistical skills. Barbarian sieges of Roman fortified sites often collapsed after a few days. A city might fall if surprised by a fast barbarian raid, as Nova Epirus fell in 479 AD. Another possibility is that some sort of ruse might be used to get warriors into the city to open a gate. In 378 AD Goths tried to infiltrate Roman deserters into Adrianople but the city held despite the defeat of the mobile army. One way barbarians captured a walled city was by treachery. Some ordinary Roman citizens had more sympathy with the barbarians than their own ruling classes.

Barbarians almost never used siege engines during this era. Ladders represented the peak of barbarian technology. One exception was the army of Attila the Hun, which used battering rams and 'shields', modest equipment by Roman standards. Even this capability disappears after the dissolution of Attila's army and the suspicion is that Roman deserters in the warlord's personal retinue were responsible.

EQUIPMENT

Bows were used infrequently except by those barbarians from the steppes, notably the Huns, who used composite-bow armed horse archers. Long bows of 1.5m in length have been found but to postulate long bow armed units would be stretching the evidence. The use of slings also appears to have been rare. A wide variety of javelins were used and this was a common missile weapon.

Throwing spears were a favourite weapon of the troops. A number of barbarian missile weapons can be classed as heavy throwing spears. *Angons* (the barbarian pila) were widely used. *Franciscas*, throwing axes, are usually associated with the Franks but they have been found all over the Barbaricum. Similarly, the *sax*, a single-edged, pointed long knife from which the Saxons are supposed to have derived their name, was widely distributed.

Spears, 2.5m-3.5m long were the standard melee weapon for both infantry and cavalry whilst saxes were the common hand weapon. Swords were rare and used mostly by nobility (including the shock cavalry). They were long, 1m, double edged cutting weapons resembling the *spatha*. The heavy shock cavalry of the Eastern barbarians used a *kontos*, a thrusting spear. Lassoes were an unusual weapon also associated with steppe cavalry.

The primary defensive equipment of barbarians were shields. Armour and helmets were rare and limited to nobles and comitatus, who were mostly mounted.

A chance encounter (Roman cavalrymen meet their new mount!)

·THE·WARLORDS·

The 5th century was a time of warlords. The lives of five are discussed on the following pages because between them they seem to sum up the era. Others could have been chosen, for example, Theoderic, Ricimer or Asper. The named warlords listed below can only be used with the agreement of both players.

FLAVIUS STILICHO & ALARIC

Stilicho's father was a Vandal who commanded some Vandal foederati units for Rome at the Battle of Adrianople. His father was, therefore, a senior Roman officer and he married a Roman lady from a family appropriate to his rank. Stilicho came from a very important family. When Stilicho was still young, he was sent as the Emperor's representative in 384 AD on an important diplomatic mission to Persia concerning *'The Armenian Question'*. The mission must have been successful, possibly he found the answer to the question, because upon his return to Constantinople he married the Imperial Princess Serena and was promoted *Comes Sacri Stabuli*.

Stilicho then received more promotion to *Comes Domesticorum*, the Imperial Bodyguard. In this role, it is likely that he fought with Theodosius in the war against the British rebel Maximus. He must have impressed his superiors, as a further promotion to *Magister Utriusque Militae*, one of the five Field Marshals of the East, soon followed. This gave him an important military role at the Battle of the Frigid River. He had an ally there, the barbarian leader Alaric.

Alaric's early life is unclear – the barbarians were not noted for assiduously compiling records. He might have been with Fritigern at Adrianople but he would have been young, maybe even a child in the wagons although it is possible that he fought as a young warrior. Alaric was from the Balthi family and hence a regales. He attended a Roman military academy and was certainly a (the?) senior commander of Theodosius' allied barbarian forces at Frigid River and about this time became 'King of the Visigoths'. Legend has it that Stilicho was Alaric's commander and that he ordered the Visigoth to lead a suicidal attack through a pass assailed by enemy soldiers on all sides. Another story suggests that Alaric and Stilicho became firm friends.

The death of Theodosius greatly complicated Stilicho's life. He became guardian to Honorius, the new Western boy emperor, who married Stilicho's daughter, Maria. Theodosius' daughter, Galla Placidia, was entrusted to Stilicho and Serena, and was engaged to their son, Eucherius. Stilicho, in short, was well connected and became effective ruler of the West.

Unfortunately, he also claimed that Theodosius in addition had secretly charged him with the guardianship of the Eastern boy emperor. This brought Stilicho into conflict with Rufinus, Praetorian Prefect and effective ruler of Constantinople.

Alaric, meanwhile, was snubbed in his attempt to obtain official recognition as a Roman army officer. Furious, and still bitter about Gothic losses at Frigid River, Alaric led the allied Visigoths within the Empire on plundering raids in the Balkans. Stilicho withheld part of the Eastern army in the West, exacerbating the situation.

Finally, Stilicho acted and marched elements of the Eastern and Western mobile armies to confront Alaric in 395 AD. Stilicho cornered Alaric in northern Greece and a major clash of arms between Roman and Gothic warlords seemed inevitable. Alaric was expected to lose but the German king then made the first of a miraculous series of escapes.

A jealous Rufinus persuaded Arcadius to order Stilicho to return the Eastern units and withdraw to the Western Empire. Stilicho obeyed and his motivation for this is impossible to reconstruct at this distance. He may have hoped to advance his personal ambitions with Arcadius by obeying, or he may have hoped that Alaric's activities would force Arcadius to beg for help from the West. One little indication of Stilicho's aims are that the Eastern Roman units that he returned to Arcadius promptly murdered Rufinus upon reaching Constantinople.

If Stilicho thought he was to replace Rufinus he was to be disappointed. The advisor who gained control of Arcadius was the Lord Chamberlain, a eunuch called Eutropius. Alaric moved down into Greece in 397 AD, plundering and destroying in true barbarian style. Famous cities like Megara, Corinth, Argos and Sparta were sacked. Again Stilicho moved east, cornering Alaric in the Peloponnese near the site of the Olympic Games. The eunuch leader of the East was busy having Stilicho declared a public enemy and again Stilicho was ordered out of Byzantine territory. Astonishingly, again he went. The wily Alaric escaped north, supposedly over the frozen Gulf of Corinth.

Eutropius persuaded the *comes* of Africa, Gildo, to revolt in 397 AD and transfer allegiance to Byzantium. Stilicho supplied the West with grain from Gaul and Spain for the duration of the emergency and in 398 AD despatched an army of 5,000-10,000 elite Western troops to Africa under Gildo's brother, Mascezel. Gildo crumbled without a fight. Legend insists that a jealous Stilicho murdered Mascezel as a reward for his loyalty.

Eutropius, meanwhile, had arranged successful campaigns against Hun raiders and proposed to reward himself with a consulship. However, Constantinople was not yet ready for a eunuch consul and Eutropius fell.

Anti-German feelings were running high in Constantinople. A popular militia cornered a barbarian leader called Tribigild and his men. Tribigild escaped when a German called Gainas, who was *Magister Militum In Praesenti* commanding the units returned by Stilicho to the Eastern army, came to his aid. Gainas, supported by Arcadius' wife, persuaded the Emperor that Tribigild had been ill-treated by the eunuch. For a short while Gainus was the power behind the throne but popular resentment forced him to flee to the Danube where Uldin, King of the Huns, relieved him of his head.

Some time before 400 AD, Alaric got the Roman military command he wanted – *Magister Militum per Illyricum*. This gave him access to Roman arsenals but by 401 AD he seems to have sucked them dry. His horde took to the road and headed for Italy while Stilicho was crushing a barbarian incursion to the north in Raetia. The Visigoths plundered northern Italy, capturing a number of cities including Aquileia. The key city of Milan lay in his path.

Stilicho assembled a mobile force from as far afield as Britain and recruited Vandal and Alan allies. He raced south and stormed Alaric's position in a night attack, relieving Milan. Alaric moved south-west to Pollentia and regrouped. On Easter Day, 402 AD, the armies met. The cautious Stilicho intended to wait for reinforcements and crush Alaric utterly but his rash barbarian allies took matters into their own hands.

The Alan cavalry launched a furious assault that was promptly repulsed by the Goths. A no doubt cursing Stilicho committed his Roman infantry to rally the Alans. After a raging battle, the Goths were broken but Alaric pulled off one of his disappearing tricks while the Romans pillaged the captured Visigoth camp and retreated back to the Eastern Empire. Stilicho captured Alaric's wife and pursued the King catching up with him at Verona. The armies clashed and

again Alaric was defeated but with great skill extracted the survivors and retreated back to Illyricum to lick his wounds.

Another Gothic warlord, Radagaisus, assembled an army of barbarians, slaves, bacaudae and Roman deserters in 405 AD. He crossed the Danube into Italy with 20,000-40,000 men and marched south to Florence. Stilicho arrived with a force of 20,000 including Hun and Alan allies and drove Radagaisus' army into the Fiesole Highlands. He trapped them there, starved and then annihilated them. Thousands of men were captured and pressed into the Roman army. Radagaisus was captured and ceremonially executed in Rome; just like the good old days! Stilicho and Alaric were now the premier warlords of the Roman world. There was no one to touch them, but Stilicho's doom was coming.

The winter of 406 AD was cold and the Rhine froze. Too many of the mobile armies from Britain and Gaul had been sucked into Italy by the Alaric crisis. On the last day of the year a huge migration of Vandals, Alans and Suebi crossed the river and swept like a plague across northern Gaul. Stilicho was absorbed by his claims in the East. Britain rebelled and eventually the troops proclaimed Constantine Emperor and he led much of what was left of the British army into Gaul to confront the barbarians. Stilicho despatched Sarus who unsuccessfully challenged the British army, not the barbarians. Stilicho's next reaction was to pay Alaric, who demanded 4,000 pounds of gold, to march west as an ally, not against the Vandals but against Constantine. Stilicho seriously proposed to arrange for a barbarian army to destroy the last effective Roman army in the Western Dioceses.

In 408 AD, Arcadius died. Stilicho proposed to travel to Constantinople to advance his Eastern ambitions and leave the West to the tender care of Alaric. It was too much. The army disowned their disgraced leader. The Magister Scrinii Olympius led a coup. Stilicho fled to a church in Ravenna but was executed on 13th August, 408 AD.

An anti-German pogrom followed Stilicho's fall. Some 30,000 allied barbarian troops marched out of Italy to join Alaric. The Visigothic warlord reinvaded Italy in 408 AD, with Stilicho dead there was no one who dared or was willing to oppose him. Supposedly he heard voices saying '*You shall enter the city.*'. The horde moved on Rome down the via Flaminian Way. Alaric captured the port on the mouth of the Tiber, cutting Rome off from North African grain. The city starved.

Fearing treachery, the Senate murdered Serena, Stilicho's widow. Alaric offered terms which were '*beyond even the insolence of a barbarian*' (Zosimus). He demanded all the citizens' gold, silver, portable treasure and all the Germanic slaves in the city. When a Roman delegate pointedly asked what he intended to leave behind, Alaric quite reasonably replied '*Your lives.*'. The Romans were so terrified that Pope Innocent considered allowing pagan rituals to attract the attention of Rome's old gods.

The Senate offered Alaric a bribe of 5,000 pounds of gold, 30,000 of silver, 4,000 tunics of the highest quality and even 3,000 pounds of spices. The deal fell through when Honorius through his unmilitary advisor, Olympius, still withheld the official Roman position and land rights Alaric desired. The siege dragged on through 409 AD.

Finally, the inhabitants of the city rebelled and in collusion with the Visigoths created a new Emperor, Attalus, who appointed Alaric, *Magister Utriusque Militum*. Attalus astonished his new general by having a mind of his own and refusing to allow the Visigoths into North Africa. The frustrated warlord deposed him and blockaded Rome in 410 AD for the third time. On the 24th August someone opened the Salarian Gate and the warriors poured in. For three days the army raped and plundered before heading south in their endless and insatiable search for food. They reached the tip of the peninsula and prepared to cross to Sicily. This was the end of the adventure for Alaric. A huge storm wrecked the Gothic fleet and the disappointed Visigoths streamed back north. Without warning Alaric died.

The Goths used slave labour to divert the River Busento. They buried Alaric somewhere in the riverbed and allowed the water to flow over the grave. The slave labourers were then murdered to preserve the secret of the location. The Goths succeeded so well that Alaric's tomb still escapes the archaeologists today.

The legacy of the two warlords is difficult to evaluate. Stilicho was a fair general, he was the only man to check Alaric, but he was a political disaster. He disunited the Eastern and Western Empires at a critical time and presided over the collapse of the Rhine frontier, the loss of Britain and the devastation of northern and western Gaul. Arguably, he was the man who lost the West.

Alaric's career also appeared to end in failure. He never did get the Imperial recognition he craved and the Visigoths were still a nomadic horde without a safe homeland. But in the long run his impact was enormous. He demonstrated the weakness of the Western Empire and almost single-handed developed the idea of German kingship and nationhood. With the Visigothic nation, he created something with a lasting impact. He was a pivotal figure in the construction of Western culture.

Stilicho, Roman Generalissimo 360–408 AD

Stilicho was a competent general but often seems to have allowed his military skills to be impeded by devious political objectives. This reduced his ability to control his forces.

	M	WS	BS	S	T	W	I	A	Ld	Pts
Stilicho	4	5	5	3	3	3	6	2	9	136
Warhorse	8	3	0	3	n/a	n/a	3	1	n/a	n/a

Equipment: Sword, light armour, shield and warhorse.

Special Rules: Any unit within 8" of Stilicho may use his Leadership value when it takes a Leadership test. Roll a D6, on a 4-6 the battle is in Stilicho's political interest, otherwise it is not. If the battle suits his political interests he gets double Victory points if the enemy commander is killed. If the battle is not in his interests and the enemy commander is killed he receives no Victory points for the death. *Drilled.*

Stilicho's bucellarii

	M	WS	BS	S	T	W	I	A	Ld	Pts
Bucellarii	4	4	4	3	3	1	4	1	8	30
Warhorse	8	3	0	3	n/a	n/a	3	1	n/a	n/a

Roman archers

Equipment: Armed with sword, shield, light armour and throwing spear.

Special Rule: *Drilled.*

Alaric, King of the Visigoths, ?–410 AD

Alaric is famous for his astonishing escapes. After many battles, a number of which he lost, he eventually died of natural causes.

	M	WS	BS	S	T	W	I	A	Ld	Pts
Alaric	5	6	6	4	4	3	6	3	8	162
Warhorse	8	3	0	3	n/a	n/a	3	1	n/a	n/a

Equipment: Sword, throwing spear, shield and light armour. Rides a warhorse.

Special Rules: Any unit within 12" of the General may use his Leadership value when it takes a Leadership test. If Alaric, and his unit, flees then they always move 18". If Alaric loses his last wound then roll a D6. On a 2+ he has escaped. Alaric is removed from the battlefield but yields only half Victory points to his opponent.

Alaric's bucellarii

	M	WS	BS	S	T	W	I	A	Ld	Pts
Bucellarii	8	4	4	4	3	1	4	1	6	30

Equipment: Armed with mixed weapons, throwing spears, light armour and shields. Mounted.

Special Rule: If Alaric is removed from the battlefield, then his bucellarii share the same fate, yielding Victory points accordingly.

FLAVIUS AETIUS & ATTILA

Aetius was born to an Italian Roman noble mother whose family had wealth and prestige. His father, Gaudentius, was a senior soldier (Master of Horse) whose family was descended from Eastern barbarians (Sarmatians or Alans). Sometime around 405 AD, the Visigothic warlord Alaric demanded two hostages of noble blood from the Romans; one of them was Aetius. This was the making of him. He caught Alaric's eye and was trained as a barbarian noble warrior. He rode with Alaric when the Visigothic warlord invaded Italy and sacked Rome. He was also with Alaric when the warlord died. Alaric was replaced by Athaulf, who negotiated a new deal with the Empire. He received the hand of the Princess Galla Placidia in marriage as a sweetener. As part of the settlement, hostages were released and in about 410 AD Aetius returned to court.

His father had died and without patronage Aetius was again sent as a hostage. This time he was despatched to the court of Charaton, King of the Huns. The young Roman once more hurled himself into barbarian life making friends among the Hunnish optimates and regales. In learning the ways of the heavy cavalryman and the horse archer, Aetius was probably acquiring the skills of his grandfather. At this court, he would have met a young nobleman whose name would forever be linked with his own, Attila.

By 420 AD, Aetius was back at Honorius' intrigue-riddled court. Honorius' warlord Constans died and fighting broke out between the bucellarii of Placidia (Constans' wife and Honorius' sister) and Honorius. Placidia was banished to Constantinople in 423 AD. A few months later Honorius died, leaving a power vacuum in the West.

Castinus, Magister, put John, the chief secretary, on the throne. Aetius, who was *cura palatii* (Palace Governor) was sucked into the plot. He was despatched to the Hungarian plains to recruit a Hunnish army. Meanwhile, the furious Placidia was riding west with her Visigothic bucellarii and a Romano-barbarian army under the Alan, Ardabur. Somehow, Aetius contrived to be three days late as John's army collapsed and the pretender was executed.

Aetius was pardoned, 6,000 armed Huns ensured that, and promoted to comes (Count) of the Imperial forces in Gaul. Aetius was now the Imperial policeman of this strategic province. He kept an eye on the Visigoths and suppressed the bacaudae. He punished Frankish raids and was so successful that by about 426 AD he was promoted to magister militum – a full warlord.

Another character now enters the story. Boniface, warlord of North Africa, was losing control of his province to local barbarians. In 427 AD he was recalled by Placidia and revolted, absorbing the Western Imperial army and the Gothic force sent to compel him. In 429 AD, the Vandals invaded North Africa and Boniface was unequal to the challenge. He returned to Placidia who, hoping to use him to tame her over-mighty warlord in Gaul, promoted Boniface to magister militum.

An incandescent Aetius rode for Italy with his Hun bucellarii. Boniface rode to confront him with his own bucellarii. South of Ravenna, at the fifth milestone beyond Rimini the warlords met. A duel between them became a full-blown battle. Boniface won but was wounded and died within a few days. Aetius was now undisputed warlord of the Western world.

Aetius, middle-aged, effectively ruled the Western Empire, the last Roman who could make this boast. When the Burgundians offended Rome in 437 AD, Aetius and his deputy Litorius led an army of Huns that destroyed their king, Gundahar, his family, and 20,000 of his followers. An event so traumatic that it passed into German mythology and provided the plot for Wagner's *Nibelungenlied*. Oddly enough, mythology transmuted the name of the enemy warlord from 'Aetius' to 'Attila'.

Times were changing in the Hun-ruled lands and Aetius' old friends were disappearing. The Huns in the west were lead by two regales, Attila and his older brother Bleda, who had welded the tribes into a single force.

In 441 AD, the pious Bishop of Margus crossed the Danube and went grave robbing from Hun noble tombs. In retaliation, the Huns raided into Roman territory demanding the surrender of the reverend bishop. The good bishop surrendered himself, presumably under a certain degree of persuasion, and promptly did a deal with the Huns. In return for his life, the noble bishop agreed to sneak into Margus and throw open the gates so that the barbarians could sack and destroy the city.

The Romans patched up a treaty by paying tribute until they had repaired the Danubian defences in 443 AD. When the treaty lapsed the brothers led the Hun on a pillage as far as the walls of Constantinople where they beat a Roman army. The Emperor bought them off with a huge ransom of 2,100 pounds of gold.

In 445 AD, Attila became king by the cunning expedient of murdering his brother. A description of Attila is given in Gibbon.

'a large head, a swarthy complexion, small deep-seated eyes, a flat nose, a few hairs in place of a beard, broad shoulders, and a short square body, of a nervous strength, though of a disproportionate form… he delighted in war; but, after he had ascended the throne in mature age, his head, rather than his hand, achieved the conquest of the north; and the fame of an adventurous soldier was usefully exchanged for that of a prudent and successful general.'

A rusty old sword was found buried and brought to the king. He promptly declared it to be the personal weapon of Mars and carried it as proof that he had the particular favour of the War God. Attila then carried out a series of attacks against the Eastern Empire in the Balkans that caused terrible destruction in 447 AD. There was an earthquake that shattered even the walls of Constantinople, and then storms, plague and finally Attila. Again he smashed a Roman army sent to defeat him

In 448, a Roman delegation camped near Nis, reported that the Huns had left a ghost city, with piles of human bones scattered around. The barbarian king was forever depicted as the antichrist, with dog's ears and horns. But Roman ambassadors reported Attila as wearing simple unaffected clothes, and sitting on a wooden bench to receive them.

Gaiseric, the Vandal king in North Africa, hated the Visigoths and reportedly urged Attila to transfer his attentions westward. In 450 AD, the king of the Franks died. His younger son went to Aetius, his adopted father, for help to secure the Frankish throne. The elder son went to the only man who could hope to oppose Aetius, the Hun warlord Attila. The scene was set for a clash of titans.

Placidia sprayed a little petrol onto the flickering flames. Her daughter, Honoria, offered marriage to Attila. This seems to have been another plot by Placidia to tame her over mighty warlord Aetius. Attila was to be the new Boniface. In 451 AD, Attila led his army west across the Rhine. Placidia had died in the meantime and her son, the ineffectual Valentinian III, panicked and begged Aetius to stop the invasion.

Attila attacked the Franks in 451 AD in an effort to detach them from Aetius' sphere of influence and made overtures to the Visigoths but his diplomatic offensives were unsuccessful. Aetius built the largest army that the Western Empire had deployed for a century by creating a grand alliance that included even his old sparring partner Theoderic, the Visigothic warlord. Only the Vandals stayed aloof from the Romano-German Western alliance.

In a titanic battle, Attila was defeated in what was considered to be one of the truly decisive battles of the Western world. Aetius deliberately left the warlord a line of retreat, possibly because he did not wish to annihilate the Huns who counterbalanced the Visigoths. Did Aetius plan to bring the Huns back within the Roman fold as allies? Possibly. Aetius could have left a line of retreat simply because a cornered Attila was a highly dangerous Attila. The fact is that the Hun king retreated and never challenged the Warlord of Gaul again.

In 452 AD, Attila turned his attention to Italy. In a typical Hun attack he wreaked havoc. Aquileia was wiped from the face of the earth as if it had never been and other cities in northern Italy were also devastated. Aetius and his army stayed in Gaul. Nothing could more clearly convey the fact that Aetius was warlord of a Gaulic confederation rather than a Roman military commander of the old type. The Franks, Visigoths, Britons, etc, were not going to leave their lands unguarded to pursue military adventures in Italy. The modern boundaries of Europe were forming.

In the end, Attila's invasion was a failure. He achieved nothing of any importance. Italy was stripped of food by a famine the previous year and inevitably, plague swept through his debilitated army. Marian, emperor in Constantinople, swung an army across the Hun supply lines adding to their woes. Diplomatic entreaties from Pope Leo gave the warlord an excuse to retreat without losing face to Hungary. There he planned a new campaign against the East.

Soon Attila was dead. The legend is that he acquired a delightful new young German bride for his harem and celebrated the wedding feast with copious quantities of wine and beer. In the morning, his body was discovered cold and stiff beside the quivering, terrified girl. Supposedly, he suffered a nose bleed through sexual exertion and drowned in his own blood. A dramatic story of heavenly revenge against the 'spawn of Satan' but one may wonder whether the romantic tale hides an assassination plot.

The Hun Empire passed to Attila's sons but their Germanic subjects plotted rebellion. In 454 AD, the Huns suffered a series of defeats and disappeared from history back into the steppes. Attila had devised a new unsuccessful policy that turned the Huns from a Barbarian empire, whose warriors earned lucrative employment as Roman mercenary allies, into an invasion force. He thrust twice into the Western Empire and was forced to retreat in disarray each time, once after a smashing defeat from Aetius, formerly the Hun friend.

Two possibilities for intrigue suggest themselves. One is that after the retreat from Italy, Attila's reputation was at an all time low and that Hunnic nobles or his own sons organised his death. Aetius must still have had contacts within the horde, was he behind a plot? The big winners from the destruction of the Huns were the Germans. Was the death of Attila the first blow in the German rebellion, not merely the trigger?

The reputation of Aetius stood supreme. As the last Roman to have commanded mighty armies and humbled the greatest of the barbarians, he went to see the Emperor in Rome in 454 AD to suggest a marriage between his son Gaudentius and Valentinian's daughter. A modest request since Aetius could have seized the Western throne at any time. The weak, petulant Valentinian murdered the old man with a dagger and the help of the court chamberlain.

A few months later one of Aetius' Hun bucellarii called Optila walked up to Valentinian on the Campus Martius in Rome and struck him down with a dagger. Optila was true to his oath of allegiance not to leave his lord's killing unavenged. Valentinian's bucellarii stood and watched. Oaths of allegiance only went so far.

Without Aetius there might have been no Western civilisation. Aetius proved that a Western army could still win battles and Chalon was a battle that had to be won. Aetius is remembered as the last of the Romans. But at the head of his victorious Romano-Germanic army, he could equally be described as the first great Western feudal king. Attila was a destroyer, he destroyed everything he touched including the Huns themselves. If Attila had been victorious at Chalon, he would have wrecked the West in an orgy of murder and destruction and contributed nothing. Attila's reputation is well founded, fortunately his career ended in total failure.

Aetius, 390–454 AD

Aetius, friend of the Huns, was noted for his battle cunning.

	M	WS	BS	S	T	W	I	A	Ld	Pts
General	4	5	5	3	3	3	6	2	9	155
Warhorse	8	3	0	3	n/a	n/a	3	1	n/a	n/a

Equipment: Sword & heavy armour. Rides a barded warhorse.

Special Rules: Any unit within 12" of the General may use his Leadership value when it takes a Leadership test. *Drilled. Stubborn.* In any battle, Aetius chooses whether his army has the first turn or not. Note that Aetius and his Hun bucellarii ride the finest horses and so can ignore the -1 movement penalty for barding.

Aetius' Noble Hun Bucellarii

	M	WS	BS	S	T	W	I	A	Ld	Pts
Bucellarii	7	4	4	4	3	1	4	1	6	40

Equipment: Heavy armour, shield, sword, and kontos. Ride barded horses.

Special Rules: *Drilled. Stubborn.*

Attila, King of the Huns, ?–452 AD

Attila was believed to possess the Sword of Mars, God of War.

	M	WS	BS	S	T	W	I	A	Ld	Pts
Warlord	5	6	6	4	4	3	6	4	8	175

Equipment: Sword, throwing spear, composite bow and light armour. Mounted.

Special Rules: Any unit within 12" of the General may use his Leadership value when it takes a Leadership test. Ignores -1 to hit modifier when moving and shooting. The Sword of Mars causes *fear* in enemy troops.

Attila's Hun bucellarii

	M	WS	BS	S	T	W	I	A	Ld	Pts
Bucellarii	8	4	4	4	3	1	3	1	6	40

Equipment: Armed with sword, throwing spear, composite bow and light armour.

Special Rules: Ignore -1 to hit modifier when moving and shooting. Free march move at the start of the first turn.

GAISERIC

"A man of deep thought and few words."

Jordanes

Gaiseric was born east of the Rhine in the Barbaricum. His father was a regales among the Vandals but his mother was merely a concubine. As a small child, he crossed the frozen Rhine in 406 AD with the barbarian horde led by his father, reaching Spain in 409 AD. When he was about twenty, the Vandals won a significant battle against a Roman army commanded by Castinus. Gaiseric was a proficient and experienced warrior who had survived a number of skirmishes with Roman and Visigothic forces.

The Vandals hired local shipbuilders and became successful pirates. Sometime before 429 AD the King died and was succeeded by his eldest legitimate son, a child called Gontharis. Somehow Gontharis died and Gaiseric succeeded his half brother. It was Gaiseric that led the Vandals to North Africa, the last virgin province in the West.

The warlord of North Africa was the *Comes Africae*, Boniface, who seemed to be suffering a mid-life crisis, with yearnings to become a monk. In 427 AD, Boniface had fallen out with the Empress and suffered an invasion from Roman forces determined to bring him to heel. One story is that Boniface actually invited the Vandals into North Africa as allies. If he did, then he soon regretted this rash action. The Vandals landed at Julia Traducta and devastated the countryside in an orgy of rape, torture and destruction.

Boniface's depleted army offered battle and was soundly beaten, taking refuge behind the walls of Hippo Regius where St Augustine was the bishop. The Vandals laid siege for 14 months. Eventually, Asper arrived in Carthage with reinforcements from Constantinople and Gaiseric negotiated a settlement. A crushed Boniface quit Africa for good with his bucellarii. The Vandals were legally granted all the land west of Carthage.

Like most Germanic barbarians, the Vandals were Arians and they ruthlessly suppressed Catholic culture. From the port of Hippo Regius, they indulged in piracy across the Mediterranean. Asper and Gaeseric seem to have come to some sort of understanding. Possibly, it was a deal in which Constantinople was to ignore the Vandals if they restricted their activities to the Western Empire. In 434 AD, Asper returned to Constantinople and in 439 AD Gaiseric captured the great port city of Carthage. He was now undisputed warlord of North Africa.

Soon the yards in Carthage were building a vast pirate fleet. The Vandals raided Sicily in 440 AD. Constantinople despatched a Roman fleet to Sicily in 441 AD but the expected naval clash never happened. A raid by Attila on the Balkans forced its recall. Not for the last time would the two great destroyers of the Roman world work in synchrony.

The Romans accepted reality and recognised Gaiseric as legitimate king of North Africa by a treaty in 442 AD. As part of his aspiration for legitimacy, Gaiseric accepted a Roman proposal for marriage between his son Hunneric and the Roman Princess Eudocia. Huneric was currently married to a Visigothic princess, in a diplomatic move to heal the bad relations between the great barbarian houses.

Gaiseric falsely accused the hapless young Visigothic princess of trying to murder him, mutilated her by cutting off her ears and nose, and sent her back to her father, the King of the Visigoths in Toulouse. The Romans promptly withdrew the marriage offer. Nothing indicates Gaiseric's cunning, viciousness and crass stupidity more than this incident. The Visigoths vowed destruction on the Vandals and all their works. Gaiseric is supposed to have supported Attila's invasion of Gaul. If true, it would have helped Aetius enjoy Visigothic support.

By 455 AD, Aetius and Valentinian were assassinated and the Emperor's widow was forced to marry the usurper Maximus who also married his son to the Princess Eudocia. The Vandals set sail for Rome whose terrified inhabitants stoned Maximus to death when they caught him fleeing the city. The Vandals plundered the city for a fortnight causing great destruction. Gaiseric sailed home with much booty, including the princess.

The Vandals continued their career of piracy. The Emperor Majorian built a mighty Romano-Germanic fleet and army and invaded Gaeseric's realm in 460 AD. It was a complete disaster and brought down the Emperor. Gaeseric's reply was to capture Sardinia, Corsica and the Balearics, creating a new Carthaginian Empire.

In 467 AD, a Vandal fleet raided the territory of the Eastern Empire. An outraged Leo gathered his forces in 468 AD and sent 11,000 ships and 100,000 men against Gaiseric under Basiliscus. They were joined by a Western force led by Marcellinus. A complex three-pronged strategy was evolved. Marcellinus captured Sardinia. Basiliscus sailed the main Byzantine fleet to Sicily and won a naval battle sinking 340 Vandal ships. Heracleius commanded a Byzantine army that was transported to Tripoli.

Dux and bodyguard

Heraclius then met a Vandal army on the coast. The army contained Germanic cavalry, Moorish cavalry, possibly Moorish camel cavalry and Moorish infantry. The cream of the Byzantine force were their Hun mercenaries. Heraclius was triumphant and he captured several small towns and advanced on Carthage. The situation was critical. Gaiseric bought time by offering Basiliscus a huge bribe while he prepared fireships. One night the Vandals sent in the fireships and the Byzantine fleet burned at its moorings. The invasion was over. In Sicily, Marcellinus was assassinated by a Vandal secret agent. Gaiseric had survived.

Gaiseric started a new diplomatic offensive with the emerging Germanic kingdoms, including the new king of the Visigoths. In 471 AD, Gaiseric's friend in Constantinople, Asper, and his whole family were executed by Leo. The Eastern Emperor survived him by just three years. Ricimer, the warlord of Italy, died in 472 AD. Gaiseric successfully forged a new relationship with the new Byzantine administration under Zeno.

Gaiseric died in his bed. He had outlived the Western Empire by one year. His life encompassed the destruction of the Western Roman world. As a small boy, he crossed the Rhine when the frontier collapsed and as an old man he witnessed the deposition of the last Emperor. But he is another example of a warlord whose Empire died with him. The Vandals remained parasites, pirates who created nothing. They failed to fashion a civilisation and earned their reputation. Gaiseric, like Attila, was a destroyer; just a more successful one.

The Moors revolted almost immediately and within fifty years the Vandal kingdom was history. The last king was paraded through the streets of Constantinople.

Gaiseric, King of the Vandals, 400–470 AD

Gaiseric was a vindictive man even by warlord standards. He never forgot a slight against him or forgave an insult, real or imagined.

	M	WS	BS	S	T	W	I	A	Ld	Pts
Warlord	9	6	6	4	4	3	6	3	8	170

Equipment: Armed with sword, mixed weapons and light armour.

Special Rules: Any unit within 12" of the General may use his Leadership value when it takes a Leadership test. Subject to *hatred* against his foes as described in Warhammer Ancient Battles, page 52.

Gaiseric's Moorish bucellarii

	M	WS	BS	S	T	W	I	A	Ld	Pts
Bucellarii	9	4	4	3	3	1	4	1	6	28

Equipment: Armed with sword, javelins, light armour and shield.

Special Rules: Light cavalry. Any unit may *skirmish*. Flees 4D6".

·THE·GREAT·BATTLES·

One of the more fascinating elements of historical wargaming is the recreation of great historical battles. This can give the players an insight into real events and raises wargaming from chess with toy soldiers into the category of historical simulation. It is great fun to see whether one can achieve more, or less, than the real generals did.

There are a number of problems in recreating real battles. Often they turned upon chance events, sometimes quite unlikely events. This creates a dilemma for game designers. We can force the event to happen and straitjacket the game, but this removes much of the fun for the players. Or we can allow a freestyle battle that will almost never follow the original path. This is also deeply unsatisfying. Why recreate an historical battle if we have no intention of following through the events?

The best compromise solution, pioneered by the great masters of wargaming like Charles Grant and Donald Featherstone, is to give these historical chance events a probability of happening in our wargame. Sometimes the wargame will follow history, sometimes players will be faced with new, demanding situations.

This system has a bonus. If you do better than the historical commander, then clearly you are a better general. If you do worse, then you are unluckier.

Recreating Historical Combat With Warhammer Ancient Battles

Warhammer Ancient Battles is best used for fighting smaller battles. However, most of the great battles for which we have records were large affairs, commonly with armies of 30,000 plus. It is not a good idea to use a ratio of much more than 50:1 when reducing armies for gaming otherwise units become too small. The best way to reduce the army size further is to use a unit reduction ratio. Let one unit of models represent two or more real units just as one model represents 50 real soldiers.

STRASBOURG 357 AD – ROME AGAINST THE BARBARIANS

Introduction
The Battle of Strasbourg is a classic Roman attack on a barbarian incursion. The battle was the most significant action fought in a campaign by Julian during his time at the Rhine frontier.

Strategic situation
The advancing Roman army seems to have known only the rough location of the Alamanni and had no idea of their strength. The Alamanni seem to have been equally ignorant. A Roman deserter tipped the barbarians off about the small size of Julian's force so the Germans decided to make a stand, setting a trap. The Romans caught a German scout who was 'persuaded' to reveal information about Chnodomarius's army. The Roman soldiers showed a lack of experience in wanting to fight immediately despite having marched a long way. Julian would have preferred them to rest before offering battle.

Terrain
The Germans selected a battleground where they could anchor their right flank against a watercourse lined with vegetation. Then they laid a trap amongst the undergrowth.

The forces
The Roman army had 13,000 men under the leadership of the general, Julian. It would also have had a full complement of supporting officers including Severus, who commanded the pivotal left wing.

Units probably at Strasbourg include, *Scutarii*, *Gentiles* (cavalry), *Primani* (legion), *Cornuti*, *Brachiati*, *Heruli*, *Batavi*, *Petulante* and *Celtae* (auxiliary palatines). At least one unit of heavy shock cavalry was also involved at some stage of the battle.

The *Alamanni* had, reputedly 35,000 men. Their leaders included a general, Chnodomarius, and a senior chief, Serapio. The army was mostly infantry with a small force of cavalry.

The battle
The Germans placed an ambush force in the vegetation on their right flank. Their warbands were placed in line across the centre and their cavalry and light infantry guarded the open right flank. An elite group of optimates formed a second line behind the warbands.

The Romans formed an infantry line with their best troops on the right flank. Units were held in reserve behind the main line (notably the Primani legion). The cavalry was on the open right flank.

The two sides closed and exchanged missile fire, the cunning Severus refused the left flank, suspecting an ambush. The warbands then charged the Romans. The cataphracts on the right flank broke and had to be rallied by the personal intervention of Julian. The Roman left flank smashed the failed ambush. The initial warband charge failed to break the Roman infantry centre and the optimates charged in turn, bursting through the centre of the Roman line but breaking when engaged by the *Primani*. The German army collapsed and suffered heavy losses while fleeing.

Playing the battle
The Romans must have a general and at least one other officer to represent Julian and Severus respectively. The barbarians must have a General and at least one other chief.

The two armies should be of equal points values. This gives the Alamanni army about twice as many men as the Romans (26,000:13,000) depending on the options chosen.

Marcellinus recounts how Chnodomarius dismounted before the battle. We suggest he leads a force of comitatus in the battle, in the second line. A number of other barbarian kings are listed as being present (Vestralp, Urius, Ursicinus, Suomar and Hortar) and the Barbarian player might like to use *optimates* to lead his warbands under these names. The Roman player should use veterans sparingly, Julian's army was not accustomed to pitched battles.

Historical outcome

In military terms, this was just another police action against the barbarians but there was an unexpected political outcome. Julian's prestige was enhanced and he was eventually forced or persuaded to rebel, this led to him being made emperor. As Emperor, he was far from an outstanding success, being responsible for the Persian debacle.

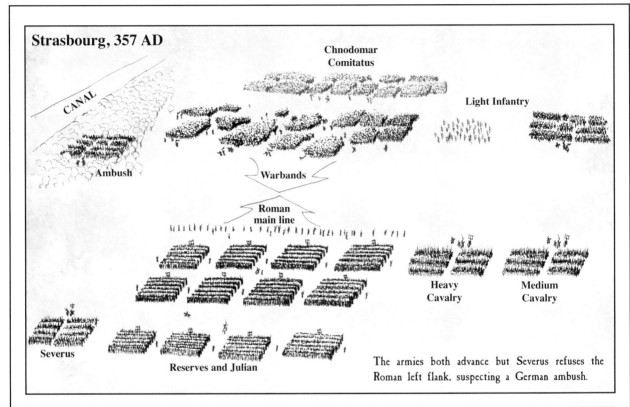

Strasbourg, 357 AD

CANAL

Chnodomar
Comitatus

Light Infantry

Ambush

Warbands

Roman
main line

Heavy
Cavalry

Medium
Cavalry

Severus

Reserves and Julian

The armies both advance but Severus refuses the Roman left flank, suspecting a German ambush.

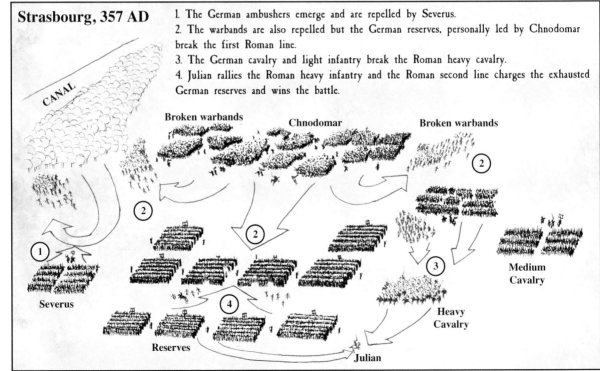

Strasbourg, 357 AD

1. The German ambushers emerge and are repelled by Severus.
2. The warbands are also repelled but the German reserves, personally led by Chnodomar break the first Roman line.
3. The German cavalry and light infantry break the Roman heavy cavalry.
4. Julian rallies the Roman heavy infantry and the Roman second line charges the exhausted German reserves and wins the battle.

CANAL

Broken warbands

Chnodomar

Broken warbands

Severus

Medium
Cavalry

Heavy
Cavalry

Reserves

Julian

THE BATTLE OF ADRIANOPLE, 378 AD – ROME AGAINST THE BARBARIANS

Introduction

The Battle of Adrianople was the greatest Roman military disaster since Cannae. More importantly, it was the first real major defeat by barbarians since the Varus disaster in the Augustine Empire. The secret was out, Rome was vulnerable. The loss of prestige was even more devastating than the loss of troops.

Strategic situation

In 376 AD, the Visigoths were driven from their lands by the Huns. The Emperor Valens gave them permission to cross the Danube into Imperial territory on condition that they gave up their weapons and became Roman farmers. The immigration was handled appallingly by corrupt Roman authorities, who treated the Goths with great cruelty. The Germans understandably rebelled, led by Fritigern, and laid waste to the surrounding countryside.

Eventually, Valens decided that the problem was sufficiently serious to warrant a praesental army. He concentrated his forces in Constantinople and then moved to the fortified city of Adrianople to await reinforcements from Gratian's Western army.

This is the point where Valens started to lose control of events. In the West, the rumour that Roman units were being posted east excited the local barbarians who promptly attacked. This delayed the Western army. Valens had received reports that the Gothic army was only 10,000 strong so he decided to offer battle without waiting for reinforcements. It is rumoured that he wished to prove his military skill by winning a battle without Gratian's help.

Terrain

The records do not suggest that terrain was an important factor in this battle so assume the battlefield is flat and unobstructed. The Goths have a wagon laager that counts as a defendable obstacle and hard cover (see page 30 of *Warhammer Ancient Battles*), in the Gothic player's half of the table.

The forces

The Romans had a praesental army of 60,000 men. The size of the Gothic force is unknown but it must have been at least as large as the Roman. Only German infantry were initially present on the battlefield, defending the wagon laager. Eventually, two cavalry forces led by Saphrax and Alatheus joined the infantry.

The battle

It was the 9th of August and the temperature was in the region of 100° Fahrenheit. Valens seems to have not had the exact location of the Gothic

army and the Romans marched in column in the shimmering heat with cavalry in the van and rearguard. At two in the afternoon the Roman column stopped to rest. After lunch it marched on, hot, thirsty and tired when it just seems to have unexpectedly bumped into the German position.

Both sides pretended to negotiate in an effort to stall the combat, the Romans needed time to deploy their force into line of battle. Fritigern too had his reasons for delay. He had been completely surprised by the sudden arrival of the Romans and all of his cavalry were away skirmishing. The astonished warlord sent mounted messengers galloping off to find the missing horsemen. Meanwhile, the Goths set fire to the dry, long grass around the Roman position to further discomfort their foes.

Eventually, the Roman army was deployed with its cavalry on both flanks. The cavalry on the left flank had the furthest distance to travel to reach its appointed position in the battleline and it arrived breathless and excited. Roman skirmishers were then sent out to harass the barbarians in their laager.

At this point Valens seems to have completely lost control of his troops who displayed the common Roman desire to get to grips with the enemy (cf Strasbourg). The skirmishers made a full blooded attack right up to the Visigothic position and the excited cavalry on the left flank followed them. Such a force had no chance of dislodging the warriors from their defensive position and they soon fell back in disarray. The warbands followed, pushing the fleeing skirmishers back on the main infantry line, causing disruption and the overextended cavalry on the left were pushed away from the Roman infantry. None of this would have been necessarily disastrous in itself but the next event spelt doom for the Roman soldiers.

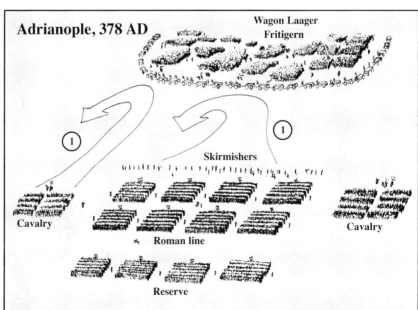

Adrianople, 378 AD

Wagon Laager
Fritigern

Skirmishers

Cavalry

Roman line

Cavalry

Reserve

1. The Roman skirmishers and cavalry launch an ill-disciplined attack on the Gothic wagon laagar and are repulsed in disorder.

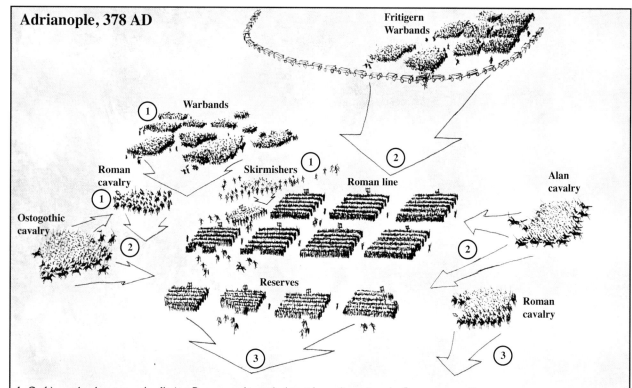

Adrianople, 378 AD

1. Gothic warbands pursue the fleeing Roman cavalry and skirmishers, disrupting the Roman centre line.

2. Ostrogothic and Alan cavalry arrive on the battlefield and attack the Roman flanks as more warbands attack the Roman centre.

3. Roman reserves and right wing panic and flee leaving this main line and left wing to be surrounded and destroyed.

The Ostrogothic and Alan cavalry forces happened to arrive on the battlefield at each flank at this critical moment. The surrounded Roman cavalry on the left flank were quickly smashed, allowing the barbarian cavalry to turn the Roman infantry's left flank. The Roman line on the left, already disrupted, was assailed by warbands in front and cavalry to the flank and rear. Despite Roman discipline, it started to crumble.

The situation would still have been retrievable if decisive action and leadership had been forthcoming. No steps were taken and soon disaster followed. The right flank cavalry fled and barbarian horsemen lapped around the right flank of the Roman infantry. Taking one look at the dire situation they were in the strategic infantry reserve fled for their lives. The Roman line was now a huddled, compressed mass. Assaulted on all sides, many of the men were too hemmed in either to defend themselves or escape.

What followed was not a battle but a massacre. Possibly as many as 40,000 Roman troops were slaughtered where they stood. Valens' bodyguard protected him for as long as they could but eventually the barbarian wave washed over his position. Valens' body was never found. One story is that the Emperor fell fighting like King Harold with an arrow through the eye. Another is that the wounded Emperor burnt to death in a cottage when it was fired by the victorious Visigoths.

Playing the battle

The two sides should be of equal points. The Barbarian army must be chosen from the Central Barbarian army list. It must be divided into three: infantry, German cavalry (ie, non-

steppe), and steppe cavalry. The infantry start the game defending the wagon laager and the cavalry armies start the battle off of the table. At the start of each of his turns, the Barbarian player rolls a D6 for each cavalry force. He adds the game turn to the dice roll. If the sum equals 7 or more then that force is placed on one of the table edges. Roll a second D6.

D6 Result

1 The Roman player selects which table edge.

2-3 The force must appear on the edge of the right flank of the Barbarian army.

4-5 The force must appear on the edge of the left flank of the Barbarian army.

6 The Barbarian player selects which table edge the force appears on.

The Gothic army is led by Fritigern, who is a general. The Roman army is led by Valens who is a senior officer, but not a general. The Roman army does not have a general. As this is a praesental army, scolae units may be used.

Historical outcome

Arguably this was the start of the rot for the Western Empire. The immediate outcome was that a Visigothic kingdom had to be accepted within the Empire. The loss of trained Roman soldiers was a considerable problem but more importantly Fritigern had displayed that full Roman armies could be destroyed by barbarians in open battle. The magic was destroyed and Roman *dignitas* (*prestige*) never completely recovered.

FRIGIDUS, 394 AD – ROMAN CIVIL WAR

Introduction

The Battle of the Frigid River came 16 years too late to be recorded in the *History of Marcellinus*, and that is greatly to our loss. It was a fascinating battle in all sorts of ways. It was the end of an era, as the last great civil war battle between the Eastern and Western armies. Interestingly, the Eastern army won which was unusual as the Western army was generally a better force. But the Battle of the Frigid River was also the first great battle of the new century as the Eastern army included a large contingent of Visigothic allies.

Strategic situation

Theodosius brought the Eastern army west to put down a Frankish magister, Arbogast, who had placed a puppet emperor called Eugenius on the Western throne. The new Western government was pagan, an intolerable challenge for the pious Theodosius. Arbogast marched the Eastern army out to meet the Easterners and they met Theodosius at the Frigid River, 35 miles from the ancient town of Aquileia inside Slovenia, near the border with modern Italy.

Terrain

The battle was fought in a wide valley where a mountain pass allowed access south from the Birnbaumer Wald. At the base of the valley runs the Wippach, the Frigid River.

The forces

The armies involved were reputedly huge, up to 100,000 troops each. In addition, Theodosius had 20,000 Visigothic allies. There were, therefore, actually three armies present, the Western Roman, the Eastern Roman and the Visigothic.

All the armies are led by generals. The Western general was Arbogast, the Eastern general was the Emperor Theodosius and the Goths had a barbarian general.

The Roman armies should be selected from the Roman army list with the exception that 10% of the points may be spent on allies from the Western Barbarian list. The Gothic army should be selected from the Central Barbarian army list.

The battle

The Western army reached the battlefield first and built a fortified palisade. On the 5th September Arbogast paraded his army in front of it and offered battle. The Eastern army reached the head of the pass by a watch tower known to the Romans as *Ad Pirum* (the pear tree). The army filed down the pass into the more open valley during the afternoon in a long column.

The Goths were in the vanguard and in the middle of the afternoon they launched a furious engagement straight from the line of march into the Western army. It is not clear whether this was the result of Gothic indiscipline or a deliberate tactic by Theodosius to: (i) cover the main Eastern army while it was deploying, (ii) try to bowl the Western army over before it was ready for battle, or (iii) to get as many Goths as possible killed while wearing down the Westerners.

If the last option was intended then the attack was a brilliant success. By nightfall the Goths took 50% casualties in a vicious and sustained frontal assault. The Western losses are not recorded but must have been substantial. That night the Western army celebrated while Theodosius prayed.

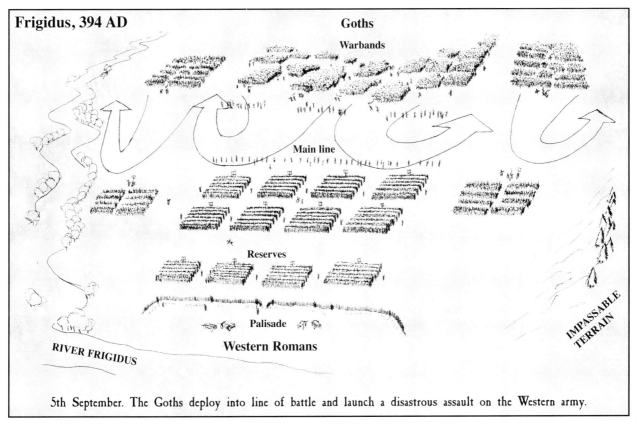

Frigidus, 394 AD

Goths

Warbands

Main line

Reserves

Palisade

Western Romans

RIVER FRIGIDUS

IMPASSABLE TERRAIN

5th September. The Goths deploy into line of battle and launch a disastrous assault on the Western army.

When morning came Arbogast was astonished to see the Eastern Roman army in battle formation. At this point some of the Western army units fled but most were steadfast. The Eastern army launched a second assault that was as bloody as the first. This time God answered and the wind known as the Bora (the north wind) came sweeping down the valley at speeds up to 125 mph. This tipped the balance and the Western army attempted to retreat to their palisade. The Easterners burnt it around them with great loss of life. The 'butchers bill' was colossal in both armies but the Western army was annihilated. Eugenius was executed whilst Arbogast committed suicide.

Playing the battle

There were three armies present, the Western Roman, the Eastern Roman and the Visigoths. Points should be allocated to the armies according to the ratio 5:5:1. Religious alignments were important, at least to the commanders. The Western army should be classed as pagan, the Eastern army as Catholic Christian and the Goths as Arian Christian. Players may wish to use priests.

All the armies are led by generals. The Western general was Arbogast, the Eastern general was the Emperor Theodosius and the Goths have a barbarian general. The Roman armies should be selected from the Roman army list with the exception that 10% of the points may be spent on allies from the Western Barbarian list. The Gothic army should be selected from the Central Barbarian army list. The Western army has a fortified palisade built behind it and the army may retreat to this.

The Frigid River is really two separate linked events and it should be wargamed in two stages. First fight the Gothic force against the Western army. The Gothic army cannot 'win' but the Eastern player's aim should be to cause as much attrition as possible to the Westerners. The second battle is between the Eastern Roman army and whatever is left of the Western. Survivors from the Gothic army may not be used by the Eastern player. Killed models and destroyed Western units are not available to the Western player. Units that fled off the battlefield on the first day might be available for action on the second. Roll a D6 for each unit, on a 4+ the unit returns sheepishly to duty, on a 1, 2 or 3 they have fled ignominiously for their lives.

The Bora wind may appear on the second day. Each turn, the Eastern player rolls a D6. If a 6 is rolled, God has answered Theodosius' prayers and the wind howls south for the rest of the game. Any unit facing the northern table edge has to add +1 to its Break rolls.

Add the Victory points from the two battles together to determine who won.

Historical outcome

The Frigid River was the swan song of the Western army. The battle led directly to the loss of the Western provinces. The losses in the army, especially the Western army, were catastrophic. The frontiers had been stripped of troops, many of which would never return. Theodosius died a few months later, worn out by the campaign, and the Empire was permanently divided between his two under-aged sons. Within twelve years, the Rhine frontier would collapse, Britain lost from the Empire, and Gaul and Spain devastated. Out of all this, the Visigoths had demonstrated a significant influence in deciding the Imperial succession and would demand further favours.

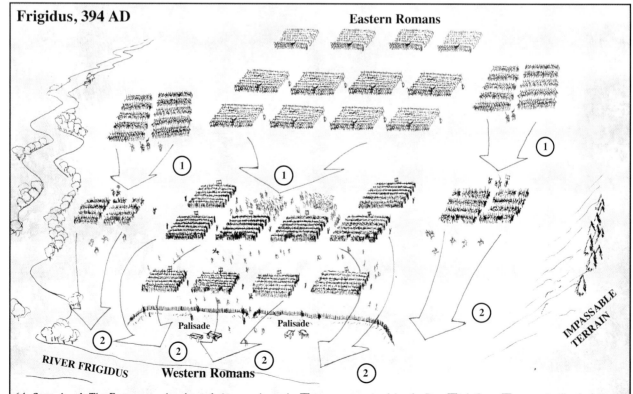

Frigidus, 394 AD   **Eastern Romans**

IMPASSABLE TERRAIN

RIVER FRIGIDUS   Palisade   Palisade   **Western Romans**

6th September. 1. The Eastern army launches a furious attack on the Western army, assisted by the Bora Wind. Some Western units flee back to the palisade. 2. The Western army break and tries to reform behind the palisade. The Eastern army burns down and overruns the Western defences.

THE BATTLE OF CHALONS
451 AD - ROME AGAINST THE BARBARIANS

Introduction

The Battle of Chalons is probably the best known and most important battle fought by the army of the late Western Empire; a gigantic tussle between the warlords Aetius, the last of the Romans, and Attila, the scourge of God. The players may wish to use the special rules for the two warlords and their faithful bucellarii.

Strategic situation

Attila crossed the Rhine in the spring of 451 AD leading a massive army from the Hun Empire. His objective was to acquire half of the Western Empire, which he considered his by right of his engagement to Honoria, Valentinian's sister. Attila was opposed by Aetius, the Roman warlord of Gaul. The warlord, with great political skill, cemented together an unlikely Romano-German alliance. But Attila rapidly captured Metz, Rheims, Mainz, Strasbourg, Cologne, Worms and Trier.

He then besieged Orleans until threatened by the advancing allied army. Attila retreated to the open countryside and offered battle on the Catalaunian Plains in Champagne. Attila seems to have been uncharacteristically nervous of battle and skulked in his wagon laager. He deployed his forces for battle in the late afternoon.

Terrain

The battle was fought on flat plains, probably on the left bank of the Marne. The only terrain of note was a hill. In the various suggested recreations of Chalon, this hill wanders around the battlefield as if powered by a High Elf Mage (surely wrong Warhammer? Ed.). We have followed Ferrill and placed it on Attila's right flank, near the river. Attila deployed to the south with his right flank towards the Marne.

The forces

The forces involved are reputed to have been huge, possibly as large as 100,000 men, and appear to have been evenly matched. Attila deployed his Huns in the centre of the line. On the right flank he positioned a number of German subjects from the Hun Empire. These included a large force of Gepids, so the right flank was commanded by the Gepid king Adaric. The left flank were Ostrogoths from the Hun Empire, commanded by the Ostragothic nobles, Theodemir, Valamir and Videmir.

The allied line consisted of Visigoths on the right flank commanded by the Visigothic king, Theodoric. Thorismund, who was Theodoric's son, led the Visigothic cavalry. The Alans, who were considered unreliable allies, were placed in the centre and were led by their King Sangiban. Aetius commanded a Romano-Frankish force on the left flank. Meovech, the king of the Salian Franks, led the Frankish contingent.

The battle

The hill on the flank of the Roman army was of clear strategic importance to both sides and battle commenced with each army launching their assaults upon it. The Romans forced Attila's German units back and took possession of this commanding ground. Attila's Huns, who represented the elite of his army, launched a frontal assault against the unenthusiastic Allans, driving them back with heavy losses. Both sides had attacked the weak link in the other's line with some success.

Meanwhile, Theodoric launched his Visigoths against Attila's Ostrogoths. It is clear that Aetius' battle plan was to push back Attila's wings and double envelop the Huns as they forged ahead in the centre against the expendable Alans. This was hauntingly similar to Hannibal's battle plan at Cannae.

The pivotal phase of the battle then occurred. Attila skilfully disengaged from battle and struck hard against the flank of the advancing Visigoths. His aim was to smash one of the pincers closing in on his army. The fighting was vicious. Initially, the Huns pushed back the Visigoths, slaying Theodoric, their king. But rallying, the indomitable Visigoths counter attacked and regained the lost ground.

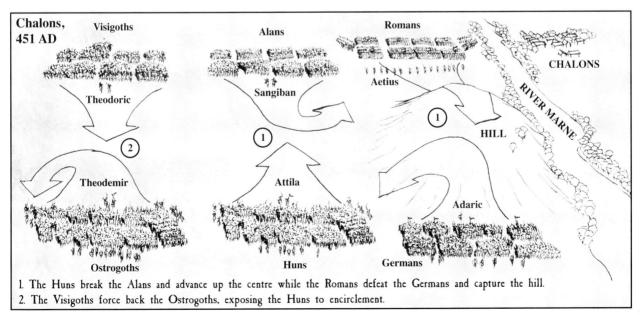

Chalons, 451 AD

1. The Huns break the Alans and advance up the centre while the Romans defeat the Germans and capture the hill.
2. The Visigoths force back the Ostrogoths, exposing the Huns to encirclement.

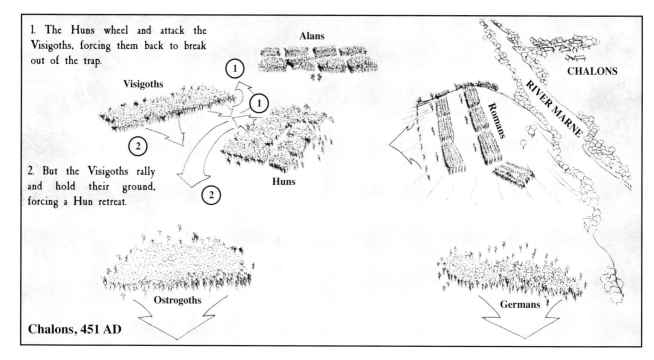

1. The Huns wheel and attack the Visigoths, forcing them back to break out of the trap.

Alans

Visigoths

CHALONS

RIVER MARNE

Romans

2. But the Visigoths rally and hold their ground, forcing a Hun retreat.

Huns

Ostrogoths

Germans

Chalons, 451 AD

Meanwhile, Aetius' Franco-Roman battle continued to advance and work its way around the German warriors making up the battle on Attila's right flank. The Hun warlord's gamble had failed and his army was in danger of encirclement and destruction. Night was falling and Attila sensibly extricated his army and retreated in good order back to his wagon laager.

Playing the battle

The playing area is a simple plain with a hill on the Roman left flank. The armies should be of equal points. It was a large battle so armies of 3,000 points are recommended. Each army breaks down into three 'battles', of which each should be allocated roughly equal points. Both armies should be chosen from the Warlord army list.

The Huns' central battle is commanded by Attila the Hun. You may use the special statistics for Attila and his bucellarii from the Warlord section. The Hun force on the right flank is commanded by the regales Adaric who is a Senior Barbarian Chief. The force on the left flank is commanded by the regales Theodemir who is also a Senior Barbarian Chief.

The Franco-Roman battle on the Roman left flank is commanded by Aetius in person. You may use the special statistics for Aetius and his bucellarii from the Warlord section. The Roman battle in the centre is commanded by the regales Sangiban who is a Senior Barbarian Chief. The Roman battle on the right flank is commanded by the regales Theodoric, who is a Senior Barbarian Chief.

The unenthusiasm of the Huns' German allies under Adaric and the Romans' Alan allies under Sangiban was an important feature of the conflict. These units in these two battles add +1 to any Break or Panic tests.

Chalons can also be recreated as a much bigger battle using three tables and three players per side. The tables represent the centre and two wings of the battlefield. The forces consist of three subunits of equal size as above but now each 'battle' is an army in its own right, led by a general. One player on

each side takes the role of the supreme commanders, Aetius and Attila. The two supreme commanders allocate one of their armies to each table in secret. Three separate battles are now fought. Players can move a unit off the appropriate side of a table, onto the corresponding side of an adjacent table. The unit must spend one full turn 'off table' representing marching between the combat zones.

Two players can also recreate Chalons as a campaign. This is a particularly good way for two players to recreate a huge battle with limited availability of models. Each player designs three armies as above and allocates each army to a 'table' in secret. Then the two armies led by Attila and Aetius must fight their respective opposite numbers on their tables. If by chance they end up facing each other then they fight to conclusion and the winner has won the entire battle. It is assumed that allies will run away if their warlord is defeated. But if they face one of their opponent's allied armies then they fight them as self-contained battles. Again, if one of the warlords is beaten then he has lost the game and his opponent is triumphant – in the unlikely event of both losing, the game is a draw. If both warlords win they may take half their surviving units and add them to an allied army. A new round of combat commences. This is repeated until one or both warlords is defeated and a conclusion reached.

Historical outcome

Aetius allowed the defeated Huns to withdraw from Gaul. This was probably to avoid risking a second battle where the favourable outcome of the first might be overturned. Attila was still dangerous. The Huns never returned to Gaul and the Battle of Chalons ranks as one of the most decisive battles in European history, as important as Marathon or Normandy. Chalon decided that the culture of Western Europe and the American colonies would be Latino-Germanic. Aetius 'the last of the Romans' had won

'The last victory which was achieved in the name of the Western Empire'

Gibbon

·CAMPAIGNS·

After a while, fighting one-off battles starts to pall and the fresh edge of excitement fades. It is now that the truly dedicated wargamer's mind turns to campaigns. These are a way of linking scenarios together so that the outcome of one battle affects the composition of the next. The simplest form of campaign is the 'linked scenario system'. This system has the advantage of not requiring an umpire. A simple campaign to get you started is described below but we strongly recommend you devise your own. It really does open up a new level of interest in wargames.

This section describes a number of scenarios. Together they allow you to fight various stages of an escalating border incident, starting with a raid on a local village by barbarians, or a Roman raid on a village loyal to the enemy during a civil war.

Not all of these scenarios are full-scale battles, a number of them are only small skirmishes involving a handful of troops on each side. Players should note that these scenarios are not fairly balanced, but who ever said war was fair!

Armies are chosen from the army lists with any extra restrictions or rules mentioned in the Scenario special rules.

THE CAMPAIGN

The following scenarios can be played as stand alone battles but to play a campaign with the outcome of each battle affecting the next, use the rules below.

Scenario 1

If the attacker wins, then play Scenario 2. The winner of the first game is the attacker. If the defender wins then play Scenario 1 again. This time roles are reversed as the original

defender takes his revenge on the attacker. If the attacker wins, play Scenario 2. If the defender wins, play Scenario 1 again with roles reversed. This continues until an attacker wins.

Scenario 2

Play Scenario 3. The winner of Scenario 2 becomes the attacker in Scenario 3 as the defender's garrison had no warning of the impending attack.

Scenario 3

Play Scenario 4.

Scenario 4

If there is a winner, play the Pitched Battle from *Warhammer Ancient Battles*, the winner of Scenario 4 takes the first turn. If Scenario 4 was a draw then play the Meeting Engagement from *Warhammer Ancient Battles*.

Pitched Battle or Meeting Engagement

We recommend a force of between 1,500 and 2,000 points for this battle. The proceeding battles, Scenarios 1-4 have an affect on the army available to a player, as follows:

(i) Scenario 1 = Losing army deducts 1D6x15 points.

(ii) Scenario 2 = Losing army deducts 1D6x25 points.

(iii) Scenario 3 = Winning army may use up to 20% of their army as a flanking force which arrives on the table from Turn 2 on a D6 roll of 4+. Roll each turn until the flanking force arrives.

(iv) Scenario 4 = Losing army deducts 1D6x12 points of cavalry allowance.

Huns attacking

SCENARIO 1 – BORDER RAID

The campaign starts

Towns and villages along the borders of the Empire can be risky places to live. They are always the first target of any barbarian incursion or the objective of some upstart would be emperor wanting to make his mark. The combatants involved in these raids are usually of drastically differing quality – on one side hand picked, well equipped troops or raiders, and on the other, desperate men and women defending their homes with pitch forks and broomsticks.

Fighting the scenario

This scenario is an encounter between two forces as described above. The raiding party is the attacker and the villagers the defender.

Objectives

The attacker's objective is to kill or drive off the table half of the villagers. The building rules are on page 69 of *Warhammer Ancient Battles*. The defender's objective is to stop this happening.

The battlefield

The setting for this raid is a small village of between three and five buildings somewhere on the Empire's border. Players should set up the village in the middle of the table at least 12" from any table edge.

Special rules

The scenario is played using normal Warhammer Ancient Battles rules with the following exceptions:

Commanders: The character with the highest Leadership counts as General of his own side. Any models within 12" may use his Leadership value in the same way as an army general.

Independent models and units: Use the skirmish rules, described in the Skirmish section, for this scenario.

Special deployment: Only troops on the attacker's side may use any special deployment rules.

Deployment

The defender deploys first anywhere inside the village. The attacker then chooses a table edge and deploys 6" from the edge.

First turn

The attacker has the first turn.

Game length

The game lasts until the attacker completes his mission or is destroyed.

Attacking force

The raiding party consists of a maximum of 300 points chosen from the following list:

Raid commander: The raid commander may be any character allowed to your army except for a General/Warlord or Battle Standard/Warbanner.

0-6 Mounted troops: Any cavalry available to your army, but no troops wearing heavy armour.

0-30 Infantry: Any infantry available to your army.

Defending force

The village militia consists of a maximum of 300 points chosen from the following list:

Village chief or leader: The raid commander may be any priest or infantryman available to your army.

0-30 Villagers: Must be Militia for a Roman army, Warriors for a Barbarian army and can be either for a Warlord army.

SCENARIO 2 – TESTING THE DEFENCES

The first real battle

Despite the defender's best efforts at patrolling the local area, the attackers have managed to sneak up on the local defence force (either the Roman limitanei or a local regales with his warriors).

Fighting the scenario

This scenario is a battle between two small armies, led by a senior commander from each side. The attacker is the winner of the first scenario, the defender is the loser.

Objectives

The attacker's objective is to destroy the local army, thereby denying intelligence to the main enemy army when it arrives.

The battlefield

The battle is set in a suitable site not far inside the defender's territory. Players should set up scenery to represent the area being fought over.

Special rules

The scenario is played using normal Warhammer Ancient Battles rules with the following exceptions:

Commanders: The character with the highest Leadership counts as General of his own side. Any models within 12" may use his Leadership in the same way as an army general.

Deployment

The defender deploys first, 12" in from his table edge. The defender may have up to 24" of palisade to put around their camp. The attacker then deploys 2D6 +12" in from his table edge. This represents the army advancing under cover of darkness and launching the attack at dawn.

Palisade

Models defending from behind a palisade have the advantage of a defended obstacle. Only infantry can defend from behind a palisade.

First turn

The attacker has the first turn.

Game length

The game lasts four turns.

Attacking force

The attacker's army consists of a maximum of 750 points chosen from the following list:

Senior commander: The senior commander may be any character allowed to an army except for a General/Warlord or Battle Standard/Warbanner.

0-2 Units of cavalry: Any cavalry available to the army, but not comitatus or any troops wearing heavy armour.

1 + Units of infantry: Any infantry available to your army, but not comitatus.

Defending force

The garrison consists of a maximum of 500 points chosen from the following list:

Garrison commander: The garrison commander may be any character allowed to your army except for a General/Warlord or Battle Standard/Warbanner.

O-2 Units of cavalry: Any cavalry available to your army, but not comitatus or any troops wearing heavy armour.

1+ Units of infantry: Any infantry available to your army, but not comitatus

A river crossing

SCENARIO 3 - CLASH OF PATROLS

A patrol meets the enemy

Two hostile patrols or foraging parties meet unexpectedly. Both sides have only lightly armed troops. Unfortunately the armies are on the wrong side of the battlefield and must fight through each other to get a message back to their own side.

Fighting the scenario

This scenario is a battle between two small parties, led by a commander.

Objectives

Both sides must get an unbroken model off the opposite side of the table to get a message back to their commander. If both sides exit a model off the table, the side with the most models left wins.

The battlefield

The battle is set in a suitable site not far inside the defender's territory. Players should set up scenery to represent the area being fought over.

Special rules

The scenario is played using normal Warhammer Ancient Battles rules with the following exceptions:

Independent models and units: Use the skirmish rules described later in this book for this scenario.

Commanders: The character with the highest Leadership counts as General of his own side. Any models within 12" may use his Leadership value in the same way as an army general.

Deployment

Both sides deploy as normal.

First turn

Roll a D6 to see who goes first.

Game length

The game lasts for five turns.

Attacking and defending forces

Both patrols consist of a maximum of 500 points chosen from the list below:

Patrol commander: The patrol commander may be any character allowed to your army except for a General/Warlord or Battle Standard/Warbanner.

0-10 Cavalry models: Any cavalry available to your army may be taken. They may not wear armour.

Any number of infantry: Any infantry available to your army may be taken. They may not wear armour.

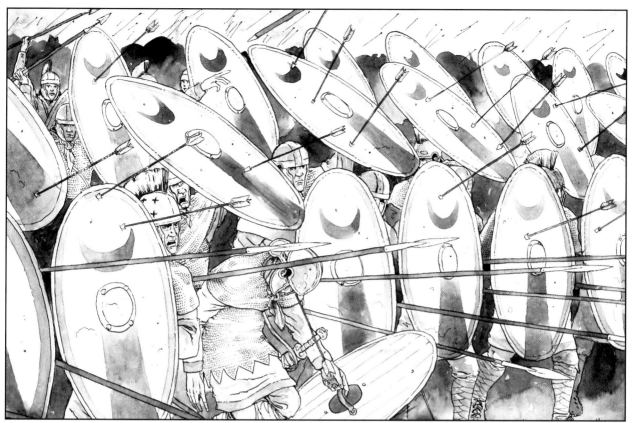

Shieldwall

SCENARIO 4 - THE MAIN FORCE ARRIVES

Find the enemy

Both generals are determined to find the enemy force before they bump into each other. To that end, both have sent out their cavalry to locate the other army. The two scouting parties meet and a vicious fight begins as each tries to buy time for its messengers to report back.

Fighting the scenario

This scenario is a battle between two cavalry patrols, led by a senior commander from each side.

Objectives

Both sides must keep all of the enemy force on the battlefield so that an enemy messenger cannot get away. To do this they must prevent a unit of five or more unbroken enemy troops from leaving the table edge that is behind them whilst trying to get a unit off their opponent's side.

The battlefield

The battle is set in rugged ground near the border. Players should set up woods and hills all over the table in groups about 18" across with 12" clear areas between them.

Special rules

The scenario is played using normal Warhammer Ancient Battles rules with the following exceptions:

Commanders: The character with the highest Leadership counts as General of his own side. Any models within 12" may use his Leadership value in the same way as an army general.

Deployment

Normal deployment rules are used.

First turn

Roll a D6 for the first turn.

Game length

The game lasts for five turns.

The winner is the side that has managed to move a unit of five or more unbroken troops off their enemy's table edge and not allowed the enemy to do the same. Any other outcome is a draw.

Attacking forces

The patrols consist of a maximum of 500 points chosen from the following list:

Senior commander: The senior commander may be any character allowed to your army except for a General/Warlord or Battle Standard/Warbanner. The commander must be mounted.

1+ units of cavalry: Any cavalry available to your army, but not comitatus or troops wearing heavy armour. If your army is not allowed to have cavalry (Sea raiders) use any light infantry.

·ARMY·SELECTION·

Three different army lists are included in this section, Roman, Barbarian and Warlord. The Roman and Barbarian armies have further subdivisions. The army lists have been created in the spirit of Warhammer Ancient Battles and are highly flexible. This is particularly true of the Warlord army. Please read the notes in *Warhammer Ancient Battles* (page 113) on how to use army lists. **Important:** Special rules for use with these army lists can be found on page 58.

The percentages given in the lists below are by points, not units or men.

ROMAN ARMY

Limitanei

Approximately 50% of a Limitanei force by unit would be cavalry, but remember that a cavalry unit was half to two-thirds the size of an infantry unit. The cavalry themselves would break down to half light cavalry and half Roman shock cavalry. It was not impossible to find a heavy shock cavalry unit amongst a Limitanei army – just very rare. The infantry would not include Palatina but might include Roman veterans and Roman Sagittarii.

Characters . . . . Up to 25%
Roman Infantry . . . . At least 25%
Roman Cavalry 20-60%
Special Units. . . . Up to 25% (with opponent's permission)

Comitatenses

Approximately one third of a Comitatenses force by unit would be cavalry, but remember that a cavalry unit was smaller than an infantry unit. Two thirds of the cavalry was Roman shock cavalry. The remainder was split between heavy shock cavalry and light cavalry.

Characters . . . . Up to 25%
Roman Infantry . . . . At least 25%
Roman Cavalry 20-50%
Special Units. . . . Up to 25% (with opponent's permission)

Note: Roman North African armies may be entirely mounted.

BARBARIAN ARMY

Sea Raiders
(Including Saxon armies in Britain)

Sea Raider armies are characterised primarily by their distinct lack of cavalry units. For some reason which remains unclear to us, Saxon armies in Britain do not seem to have created cavalry units despite having access to horse-grazing territory.

Characters . . . . Up to 33%
Barbarian Infantry . . . . The rest

Western Barbarians

The proportion of cavalry in a Barbarian army on the Rhine might vary enormously depending on circumstances but is unlikely to be much above 15% by number of men.

Characters . . . . Up to 33%
Barbarian Infantry . . . . At least 50%
Barbarian Cavalry . . . . Up to 20% (not steppe cavalry)

Central Barbarians

This type of army would have a higher proportion of cavalry than in the West with some additional steppe types.

Characters . . . . Up to 33%
Barbarian Infantry . . . . At least 25%
Barbarian Cavalry . . . Up to 40% (half may be steppe cavalry)

Eastern Barbarians

Characters . . . . Up to 33%
Barbarian Infantry . . . . Up to 25%
Barbarian Cavalry . . . Up to 100% (all may be steppe cavalry)

North African

Characters . . . . Up to 33%
Barbarian Infantry . . . . Up to 25%
Barbarian Cavalry . . . . Up to 100%

Warlord Armies

During the 5th century, barbarians flooded across the border. Gradually, the distinction between Roman and Barbarian armies broke down until a warlord's army could contain almost any mix of troops.

Characters . . . . Up to 33%
Infantry (any) . . . . At least 33%
Cavalry (any) . . . . Up to 50%

CHARACTERS

0-1 Roman Army General

A Roman or Warlord army may be led by a Roman senior commander, who represents a magister, patrician, warlord, a member of the Imperial family or even the Emperor himself.

	M	WS	BS	S	T	W	I	A	Ld	Pts
General	4	5	5	3	3	3	6	2	9	135
Warhorse	8	3	0	3	n/a	n/a	3	1	n/a	n/a

Equipment: Sword.

Options: May ride a warhorse (+3 pts). May have light armour (+3 pts), shield (+ 1 pt) or large shield (+ 3 pts).

Special Rules: Army General. Any unit within 12" of the General may use his Leadership value when it takes a Leadership test. *Drilled. Stubborn.*

0-1 Barbarian Warlord

A Barbarian or Warlord army may be led by a Barbarian Senior Chief, who represents a powerful regales or warlord.

	M	WS	BS	S	T	W	I	A	Ld	Pts
Warlord	5	6	6	4	4	3	6	3	9	145
Warhorse	8	3	0	3	n/a	n/a	3	1	n/a	n/a

Equipment: Sword and light armour.

Options: May ride a warhorse (+3 pts). May have throwing spear (+2 pts), shield (+2 pts), heavy armour (+1 pt, replaces light armour), bow (+3 pts), kontos (+3 pts) and barding (+4 pts, -1 Movement).

Special Rules: Army General. Any unit within 12" of the General may use his Leadership value when it takes a Leadership test. May be accompanied by a unit of Comitatus.

Comitatus

A barbarian chief's personal bodyguard, these were the pride of a barbarian army.

	M	WS	BS	S	T	W	I	A	Ld	Pts
Comitatus	5	4	4	4	3	1	4	1	8	13

Equipment: Armed with light armour, shields and mixed weapons, including swords, javelins and axes.

Options: May have heavy throwing spears (+3 pts), heavy armour (+1 pt, replaces light armour), bow (+3 pts), kontos (+3 pts) and barding (+4 pts, -1 Movement). Would normally be mounted (+10 pts, Movement 8).

Special Rules: Must be led by the army general. Barbarian bodyguards took oaths of allegiance extremely seriously. If the General is killed roll a D6, on a 4+ they will immediately attack the nearest enemy and are immune to Psychology and Break tests. If they eliminate their opponent, they will attack the next nearest enemy unit and so on.

0-1 Roman Army Standard Bearer

A Roman or Warlord army may have a standard representing the general's personal standard or an image of the Emperor.

	M	WS	BS	S	T	W	I	A	Ld	Pts
Bearer	4	4	4	4	3	1	4	2	8	68
Warhorse	8	3	0	3	n/a	n/a	3	1	n/a	n/a

Equipment: Sword and light armour.

Options: May ride a warhorse (+3 pts). May have shield (+ 1 pt) or large shield (+ 3 pts).

Special Rules: Any unit within 12" of the Standard Bearer may re-roll any failed Break test. *Drilled. Stubborn.*

> '**N**ow it remains for us to count, not the corpses over which we have made ourselves masters, but the living, and we have not gained conquest only to lose those whom we conquered.'
>
> Themistius 4th Century AD

0-1 Barbarian Army Warbanner

A Barbarian or Warlord army may have a warbanner representing the regales or warlord's personal banner or the totem of the canton. The banner is carried by a trusted optimates or a leader of the warlord's personal bodyguard.

	M	WS	BS	S	T	W	I	A	Ld	Pts
Bearer	5	4	4	4	3	1	4	2	8	68
Warhorse	8	3	0	3	n/a	n/a	3	1	n/a	n/a

Equipment: Sword and light armour.

Options: May ride a warhorse (+3 pts). May have throwing spear (+2 pts), shield (+2 pts), heavy armour (+1 pt, replaces light armour), bow (+3 pts), kontos (+3 pts) and barding (+4 pts, -1 Movement).

Special Rules: Any unit within 12" of the Standard Bearer may re-roll any failed Break tests.

0-1 Priest

This was a religious era and the priest figure represents the spiritual advisors attached to units or armies. Pagan or Roman Catholic Christian priests may be attached to a Roman army. Pagan or Arian Christian priests may be attached to a Barbarian army.

	M	WS	BS	S	T	W	I	A	Ld	Pts
Priest	5	3	3	3	3	2	4	2	6	75

Equipment: Hand weapons.

Options: None.

Special Rules: Any unit that includes a pagan priest *hates* all its enemies. Any unit that includes a Catholic priest *hates* enemies who are pagans or Arian Christians. Any unit that includes an Arian priest *hates* enemies who are pagans or Catholic Christians. If an army includes a priest, his opponent must declare a religious alignment (see above).

Senior Roman Officer

Roman units had senior officers, comes, dux, etc, to assist the general and command units, brigades or small armies.

	M	WS	BS	S	T	W	I	A	Ld	Pts
Officer	4	5	5	3	3	3	6	2	9	110
Warhorse	8	3	0	3	n/a	n/a	3	1	n/a	n/a

Equipment: Sword.

Options: May ride a warhorse (+3 pts). May wear light armour (+3 pts).

Special Rules: *Drilled. Stubborn.*

Senior Barbarian Chief

Barbarian units had sub-regales that would command key units or parts of a warlord's army, or command a small army in their own right.

	M	WS	BS	S	T	W	I	A	Ld	Pts
Sub-regales	5	6	6	4	4	3	5	3	8	115
Warhorse	8	3	0	3	n/a	n/a	3	1	n/a	n/a

Equipment: Sword and light armour.

Options: May ride a warhorse (+3 pts). May have throwing spear (+2 pts), shield (+2 pts), heavy armour (+1 pt, replaces light armour), bow (+3 pts), kontos (+3 pts) and barding (+4 pts, -1 Movement).

Special Rules: None.

Army Selection

Junior Roman Officer

Junior officers, praepositus, commanded Roman units. Although all Roman units had a commander, in Warhammer the officers represented here are unusually significant leaders.

	M	WS	BS	S	T	W	I	A	Ld	Pts
Praepositus	4	4	4	3	3	2	5	2	8	55
Warhorse	8	3	0	3	n/a	n/a	3	1	n/a	n/a

Equipment: Sword.

Options: May ride a warhorse (+3 pts). May have light armour (+3 pts).

Special Rules: *Drilled. Stubborn.*

Barbarian Chieftain (Optimates)

Barbarian optimates could be attached to barbarian units as leaders.

	M	WS	BS	S	T	W	I	A	Ld	Pts
Optimates	5	4	4	4	3	2	4	2	8	50
Warhorse	8	3	0	3	n/a	n/a	3	1	n/a	n/a

Equipment: Sword and light armour.

Options: May ride a warhorse (+3 pts). May have throwing spear (+2 pts), shield (+2 pts), heavy armour (+1 pt, replaces light armour), bow (+3 pts), kontos (+3 pts) and barding (+4 pts, -1 Movement).

Special Rules: None.

ROMAN INFANTRY

Pedes

These are the 'poor bloody infantry' of a Roman army.

	M	WS	BS	S	T	W	I	A	Ld	Pts
Pedes	4	3	3	3	3	1	3	1	7	8

Equipment: Armed with large shield, sword and throwing spear.

Options: May be equipped with light armour (+2 pts), javelins and darts (+2 pts), may replace throwing spear with heavy throwing spear (+1 pt). One unit may *skirmish*. Skirmishers replace their normal equipment with shield, hand weapon, javelins and darts, and may not take any other options. One soldier in four may replace the throwing spear and shield with a bow (+1 pt) but may not take any other weapons options except light armour.

Special Rules: Archers would normally be deployed at the rear of the unit (see *Warhammer Ancient Battles*, page 23). Can form shieldwall. May be *drilled* (+1 pt).

Palantina

Palatine troops were originally the Emperor's personal force. They were trained and armed much as ordinary Roman soldiers but had higher status.

	M	WS	BS	S	T	W	I	A	Ld	Pts
Palatine	4	3	3	3	3	1	3	1	8	12

Equipment: Armed with large shield, sword and throwing spear.

Options: May be equipped with light armour (+2 pts), javelins and darts (+2 pts), may replace throwing spear with heavy throwing spear (+1 pt). Any unit may *skirmish*. Skirmishers replace their normal equipment with shield, hand weapon, javelins and darts, and may not take any other options. One soldier in four may replace the throwing spear and shield with a bow (+1 pt) but may is unable to take any other weapons options except light armour.

Special Rules: Archers would normally be deployed at the rear of the unit (see the *Warhammer Ancient Battles* rulebook, page 23). Can form shieldwall. May be *drilled* (+1 pt).

Veterans

Veterans had experience of years of successful battles. Over that time they may well have supplemented their equipment with loot taken off the battlefield or had personal equipment made.

	M	WS	BS	S	T	W	I	A	Ld	Pts
Veteran	4	4	4	3	3	1	4	1	8	15

Equipment: Armed with large shield, sword and throwing spear.

Options: May be equipped with light armour (+2 pts), javelins and darts (+2 pts), may replace throwing spear with heavy throwing spear (+1 pt). Any unit may *skirmish*. Skirmishers replace their normal equipment with shield, hand weapon, javelins and darts, and may not take any other options. One soldier in four may replace the throwing spear and shield with a bow (+1 pt) but may not take any other weapons options except light armour.

Special Rules: Archers would normally be deployed at the rear of the unit (see the *Warhammer Ancient Battles* rulebook, page 23). Can form shieldwall. May be *drilled* (+1 pt).

Roman Sagittarii

These troops equipped specialist archer units.

	M	WS	BS	S	T	W	I	A	Ld	Pts
Sagittarii	4	3	3	3	3	1	3	1	7	9

Equipment: Armed with bow and sword.

Option: May take light armour (+2 pts).

Special Rules: Light infantry.

Militia or Bacaudae

Roman citizens in arms. They were untrained, badly equipped and of decidedly dubious morale. They desperately needed leadership.

	M	WS	BS	S	T	W	I	A	Ld	Pts
Militia	4	2	2	3	3	1	3	1	5	3

Equipment: Armed with hunting gear, farm tools and other sharp implements from the kitchen. Treat these as hand weapons.

Special Rules: Light infantry. May not have standards or musicians in the unit. May have a Roman Infantryman from one of the above types as a leader.

ROMAN CAVALRY

Roman Shock Cavalry
(includes Scutarii, Promoti and Stablesiani)

Most Roman cavalry were of this type. Their morale often proved to be less firm than the infantry.

	M	WS	BS	S	T	W	I	A	Ld	Pts
Cavalryman	8	3	3	3	3	1	3	1	6	21

Equipment: Armed with sword, shield, light armour and throwing spear.

Special Rules: May be upgraded to palantina, (+1 Ld, +1 pt). *Drilled.*

Scholae

Scolae were elite shock cavalry found in praesental armies.

	M	WS	BS	S	T	W	I	A	Ld	Pts
Scholae	8	4	4	3	3	I	4	1	8	26

Equipment: Armed with sword, shield, light armour and throwing spear.

Special Rule: *Drilled.*

Light Cavalry

Light cavalry units include Equites Sagittarii, Mauri, and Dalmatae.

	M	WS	BS	S	T	W	I	A	Ld	Pts
Cavalryman	8	2	3	3	3	1	3	1	5	14

Equipment: Armed with sword, javelins and shield.

Option: May have light armour (+2 pts). May replace javelins and shield with bow (+1 pt).

Special Rules: Light cavalry.

0-2 Heavy Shock Cavalry

Heavy shock cavalry units including Cataphractii and Clibanarii.

	M	WS	BS	S	T	W	I	A	Ld	Pts
Cavalryman	8	3	3	3	3	1	3	1	7	20

Equipment: Heavy armour, sword, kontos.

Options: May have shield (+1 pt) and barding (+4 pts, -1 Movement). One unit may replace kontos with bow (+1 pt).

Special Rules: Heavy shock cavalry fought in a dense formation and thus count their rank bonus in combat in the same way as light infantry (ie, they have a maximum rank bonus of +2). However, this comparatively dense formation also limited manoeuvrability and so this cavalry lose half their movement if they wheel more than 1" in a move. *Drilled.*

BARBARIAN INFANTRY

Warrior

Warriors make up the bulk of a Barbarian army. They were ferocious but poorly trained and equipped. If their first charge failed they were in deep trouble when facing Roman regulars.

	M	WS	BS	S	T	W	I	A	Ld	Pts
Warrior	5	3	3	3	3	1	3	1	5	6

Equipment: Armed with shields and mixed weapons including swords, javelins and axes.

Options: May replace mixed weapons with heavy throwing spear (eg, angons or franciscas) +2 pts.

Special Rules: A warrior unit may be designated as a light infantry unit and may *skirmish* at no extra points cost. Warriors are affected by the rules for Warbands as described in the Psychology section of the *Warhammer Ancient Battles* rulebook.

Note: If a character joins the unit or the army General is within 12", the unit may either use their own modified Ld value or the character's or General's Ld value. If the character's or General's Ld value is used, then it is not modified by the unit's rank bonus.

BARBARIAN CAVALRY

Shock Cavalry

Most Barbarian cavalry in Western Europe would be of this type.

	M	WS	BS	S	T	W	I	A	Ld	Pts
Cavalryman	8	3	3	3	3	1	3	1	7	20

Equipment: Armed with light armour, shields and mixed weapons including swords, javelins and axes.

Special Rules: None.

Light Cavalry

Troop type includes North African Moors.

	M	WS	BS	S	T	W	I	A	Ld	Pts
Cavalryman	8	2	3	3	3	1	3	1	5	14

Equipment: Armed with sword, javelins and shield.

Options: May replace javelins and shield with bow (+2 pts).

Special Rule: Light cavalry.

Steppe Cavalry

Steppe cavalry would normally be restricted to middle European and Eastern barbarian armies. It includes Huns and Alans.

	M	WS	BS	S	T	W	I	A	Ld	Pts
Cavalryman	8	3	3	3	3	1	3	1	7	22

Equipment: Armed with sword and bow.

Options: May have shield (+1 pt), throwing spear (+1 pt) and lassoes (+1 pt).

Special Rules: Light cavalry. Nomad cavalry.

0-2 Noble Steppe Cavalry

Found in both Central European and Eastern Barbarian armies, including the Sarmatians, Alans and Huns. Only noblemen were able to afford the expensive armour and weapons.

	M	WS	BS	S	T	W	I	A	Ld	Pts
Cavalryman	8	4	4	3	3	1	4	1	7	26

Equipment: Heavy armour, sword, kontos.

Options: May have shield (+2 pts) and barding (+4 pts, -1 Movement). May replace kontos with bow and throwing spear (+2 pts).

Special Rules: Noble Steppe cavalry armed with bow and throwing spear are Nomad cavalry. Noble Steppe cavalry armed with a kontos fight in a dense formation and thus count their rank bonus in combat in the same way as light infantry (ie, they have a maximum rank bonus of +2). However, this comparatively dense formation also limited manoeuvrability and so this cavalry type loses half their movement if they wheel more than 1" during a move.

North African Camelry

This troop type is included for North African Moors.

	M	WS	BS	S	T	W	I	A	Ld	Pts
Rider	6	2	3	3	3	1	3	1	5	16

Equipment: Armed with sword, javelins and shield.

Options: None.

Special Rules: Causes *fear* in enemy cavalry.

SPECIAL TROOPS

Roman Artillery

In this period, artillery was primarily used in sieges. It does not appear to have been employed in field battles. See Warhammer Ancient Battles, page 124 .

0-2 Currus Drepanus

The anonymous author of the *De Rebus Bellicis* invented wonderful machines to fight off Rome's barbarian enemies. One of the most interesting was a shock chariot. Hinged scythes were attached to the axles that could be lowered in combat or raised for safety in transit. The chariots were drawn by cataphracts. Three designs are known. The one below is a two-man, two-horse chariot. Other designs were one-horse or one-man, two-horse. As far as we know, they were never built, let alone used. But model converters might have fun making one. Another interesting design was a mobile ballistae mounted on a cart drawn by two barded horses.

	M	WS	BS	S	T	W	I	A	Ld	Pts
Currus Drepanus	6	3	3	4	4	2	3	4	6	80

Equipment: Hand weapons, kontos, heavy armour, bucklers, and barding (note that the statistics already include bonuses for equipment).

Options: None.

Special Rules: D3+2 automatic hits when charging in addition to normal attacks. Destroyed if breaks from close combat (it is not automatically destroyed after charging). Move as chariot (see *Warhammer Ancient Battles*, page 57).

Late Roman Armies

A mixed force of four cavalry (heavy, light, archers and cataphract) plus four infantry units and a bolt thrower.

An officer in campaign kit wearing a typical buff coloured cloak, mail and a plumed helmet.

A senior officer wearing classical bronze armour which would probably be left in barracks whilst on campaign.

The Scola Gentilium Seniorum, a guard unit of mail and scale armoured cavalry.

A unit of lacklustre limitani parade for their commanding officer in front of their town gate.

An army standard bearer carrying the image of the Emperor and wearing bronze and iron scale armour.

Pict warrior

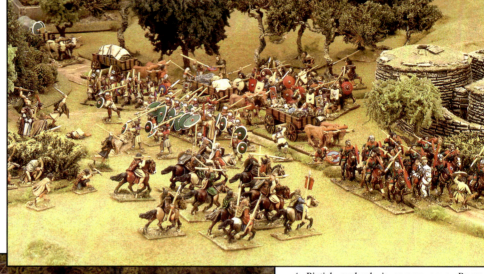

Below: A Roman column attempts to force a crossing after their signal station has been taken out by marauding Germans.

A Pictish ambush is sprung on a Roman supply column. The dilapidated broch on the right is no longer effective as a defence.

Below: A Frankish horseman hurls his angon.

The Huns 'Scourge of God' raid the Danube's frontier with Rome. They mainly attacked in a skirmish formation with the intention to hit and run

A Roman horse archer (Equites Sagittarii)

A cavalry officer of Scola Gentilium Seniorum.

A Frank and his Roman captive.

Below: A Roman villa stoutly defended by a mixed unit of Pedes, the archers trying to soften the Alammanic attack before contact.

A musician of a Roman cataphract unit. His instrument is a littus.

51

Barbarian Armies

A Frankish/Alammani raiding force of various sized infantry units and a small portion of cavalry.

Left: A unit of Ostrogoth cavalry. Mounted troops formed a larger part of Germanic forces in the east than the west.

A Frankish noble carrying a draco and wielding a francisa, the characteristic weapon of the western Germans.

Germanic warrior armed with an angon.

Mounted on a pony, this Pict uses javelins as his main armament.

A Germanic commander sporting a bejeweled and gilded ex-Roman helmet.

More and more Huns became a feature in Germanic armies and as they did so adapted to fighting in an infantry role.

The Late Roman Army

1. General (Stilicho). 2. Cataphract. 3. Senior Officer.
4. Army Standard Bearer. 5. Armoured Infantry.
6. Unarmoured Infantry. 6a. Junior Officer's helmet. 7. Limitanei.
8. Infantry Archer. 8a. Back of tunic. 9. Militia. 10. Shock Cavalryman.
11. Light Cavalryman. 12. Light Cavalryman (Moorish).

Late Roman Shields

These designs are mainly taken from the Notitia Dignitatum (a full list can be found in Phil Barker's *Armies and Enemies of Imperial Rome* by W.R.G.) except for shields 2, 5 and 6 as these are hypothetical. Feel free to make up your own patterns.

The British Army

The Gaulic Army

The Italian Army

The African Army

27. IN·NOMINE XPI SEMPER VINCAS

The British Army	**The Gallic Army**	**The Italian Army**	**The African Army**	
Cavalry	*Cavalry*	*Cavalry*	*Cavalry*	25. Dracos.
1. Honoriani Seniores.	7. Honoriani Taifali Iuniores.	13. Scola Scutariorum Prima.	19. Scutarii Seniores.	26. Gallic Limitianei Standard.
2. Cornovii Militurn.	8. Mauri Alites 'Swift Moors'.	14. Cornuti Iuniores.	20. Secundi Scutarii Iuniores.	27. Vexillums.
Infantry	*Infantry*	*Infantry*	21. Marcomanni.	
3. Invicti Iuniores Britanniciani.	9. Mattiaci Iuniores Gallicani.	15. Ioviani Seniores.	22. Armigeri Seniores.	
4. Batavi Iuniores Britanniciani.	10. Valentinanenses Iuniores.	16. Herculiani Seniores.	23. Promoti Iuniores.	
5. Caledonii.	11. Secunda Britannica.	17. Iovii Seniores.	24. Honoriani Iuniores.	
6. Cornovii.	12. Lanciarii Gallicani Honoriani.	18. Regii Seniores.		

The Barbarians

1. Gothic Noble. 2. Hun. 3. Gothic Spearman.
4. Gothic Archer. 5. Frank/Alamannic Warrior.
6. Frank/Alamannic Noble. 7. Saxon.
8. Pictish Crossbowman. 9. Vandal Noble.
10. Pictish Cavalryman.

Barbarian Shields

Barbarian shield designs are not easy to find, but this is a selection based on the few contemporary representations and general artistic styles of the period. I've included three Pictish ideas, from stone carvings, although they are mainly Germani styles. You might wish to paint whole units with the same or similar design but different colours. You may prefer to use the same colour scheme with various patterns, both methods help to tie a unit together visually and both speed up painting. Geometric patterns seem to be the most common with animalistic plaques attached to the shield occasionally appearing late in the period. This is just a guide, feel free to make up your own designs.

1. Plain wood. 2. Leather covered. 3-18. General Germanic styles.
19-20. Christian. 21. Non-Latinized Northern.
22. Possibly captured Roman. 23-25. Pictish.

·APPENDICES·

A member of the
Iovii Iuniores Gallicani

Included in the rest of this book are some additional rules and information you can use in your games of Warhammer Ancient Battles when playing with Late Roman and Barbarian armies.

Special rules: *How to use lassoes, Nomad cavalry and a few other things relevant to Late Roman and Barbarian forces in your battles.*

Skirmish rules: *The Romans and Barbarians didn't always fight in huge numbers on the battlefield so we have provided a set of rules for fighting skirmish battles using the Warhammer Ancient Battle rules. Should you need a reason to fight a skirmish we have provided some special characters and history based on the events surrounding the career of the Frankish bandit Charietto.*

The Western Empire's Order of Battle: *A disposition of forces in the Western Empire during the period covered by Fall of the West.*

How to collect an army: *Should you be torn between which army to use or want to know how to go about collecting a force we have provided some examples of sample Late Roman and Barbarian armies you could use.*

Other stuff: *Also included in this section is more history on the era, tactics and loads of useful information about books to read, details of wargaming magazines & publishers, and also addresses of societies should you want to find out about clubs and events near to you.*

·SPECIAL·RULES·

The following special rules apply to certain units in the Army lists.

LASSOES

Some steppe cavalry can use lassoes. A lasso attack is an additional special attack made by a successfully charging cavalryman before normal combat. The attacker rolls a D6 and on a 6+ the lasso attack is successful. An enemy model in base contact with the attacking model loses one attack for that round of combat. Lassoes can not be used on subsequent rounds of combat or by a model that has been charged.

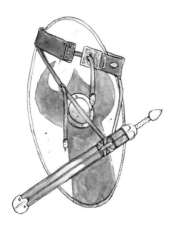

BARBARIAN CUNNING

A common barbarian tactic against enemies was to try to use rough terrain to set up an ambush on the battlefield. The Barbarian player may 'hide' a unit in a piece of suitable rough terrain on his half of the battlefield. The player writes down, or sketches, the position of the hidden unit clearly on a piece of paper. He then shows it to his opponent at an appropriate time. This keeps everyone honest.

The terrain must make a reasonable hiding place. Please do not try to claim that one's warband is cunningly concealed in a gooseberry bush. The concealed unit is revealed and placed on the battlefield at the Barbarian General's choice, or when a Roman comes within 6" of the concealing terrain. Warbands must still check for undisciplined movement (see page 53 of *Warhammer Ancient Battles*) but provided they have a character leading them they may re-roll the dice once.

NOMAD CAVALRY

In the Army lists some units of Barbarian cavalry are noted as being Nomad cavalry. The following rules apply to Nomad cavalry:

a) Nomad cavalry are allowed to make a free march move after both sides have deployed. Note that they may not use this free move to charge at the enemy, and may not shoot any missile weapons after making the move.

b) Nomadic cavalry do not suffer the -1 to hit modifier to their shooting if they moved in the same turn. However, this does not allow them to shoot if they charge or make a march move.

c) Nomadic cavalry make a normal move immediately after shooting. This is only allowed in the shooting phase, is not a charge reaction, and the unit may not have marched.

d) If Nomadic cavalry choose to *flee* or *fire & flee* as a charge reaction, they rally immediately at the end of their move, and may reform facing in any direction. This means that should the charging enemy encounter them, the Nomadic cavalry are not destroyed, and may instead fight in the close combat phase. Their opponents still count as charging.

SHIELD WALL

In the Army lists some units of Roman infantry are noted as being able to form a shield wall. They may do this instead of moving. As long as the unit is in a shield wall then all enemy attacks from the front of the unit (shooting and hand-to-hand) suffer a -1 to hit modifier. The unit benefits from the shield wall as long as it doesn't move or lose a round of close combat.

MIXED WEAPONS

In the Army lists, several Barbarian units are noted as being armed with 'mixed weapons'. Whatever the models are actually carrying they count as being armed with javelins if they are in skirmish formation and throwing spears otherwise.

Note: Astute readers will have spotted that this is a change from the mixed weapon rule in the Barbarian Army list in the Warhammer Ancient Battles rulebook. The original rule said that such units counted as having javelins no matter what their formation. The designer now feels that counting formed units as having throwing spears better reflects the way they fought. Players using the Barbarian Army list in Warhammer Ancient Battles can use this interpretation if they wish at a cost of +1 pt per model that it applies to.

"Bravery is of more value than numbers."

Vegetius

THE INCREDIBLE CAREER OF CHARIETTO

The border zones of the Roman Empire bore a striking resemblance to the Wild West. Nothing illustrates this more than the astonishing career of Charietto, bandit, bounty hunter and marshal. Charietto first emerges from the mists of the Barbaricum as a Frankish bandit raiding and looting into the Empire.

At some point, he seems to have decided that the days of easy loot were over. The future Roman Emperor Julian was kicking barbarian ass along the frontier at the time and the cunning Frank did not need a soothsayer to tell which way the wind was shifting. Charietto rode to Trier with the aim of joining the army or obtaining employment as a bucellarii or scout.

The alarmed citizens of Trier showed a marked customer resistance to his services so after some thought Charietto decided to do a little freelancing. He knew the badlands beyond the border, he knew the bandit trails and hide outs, so he decided to become a bounty hunter. It is not recorded whether he wore a poncho!

Charietto crossed the line one evening and wound his way along the secret forest paths until he reached the haunt of his old comrades. Silently, he waited for them to drink the last of the looted wine and fall into drunken oblivion. As the flames flickered on the dying ember of the fire, he strode into the camp and struck off the heads of his former friends with long slashing strokes of his spatha. After looting the bodies, he tied their heads to his warhorse to collect bounties from the local fort commander.

Mindful of the need for a positive marketing strategy, he displayed the heads back in Trier. More raids then followed and the bounties began to mount up. Soon, Charietto was accepting commissions as an agent to sort out difficulties in places that were beyond the writ of Roman law. The more prudent bandits flocked to his standard to serve as his bucellarii.

At the time, Julian was having trouble dealing with the Franks. They no longer played fair and met him in open battle where his comitatenses could pulverise them, but skulked in small guerrilla bands in the forests. Hearing of Charietto's success, Julian invited him to dinner to discuss tactics. From bandit to dinner guest at the table of the Imperial family – the lad done well! Actually, dinner with Julian was a risky business. One of Valens' generals was an Alamanni regales who had been press ganged by Julian at one of his candle-lit suppers.

A deal was struck over a charming little wine from Tuscany and Charietto became an Imperial agent. Julian's regulars swept the badlands by day, penning them into their forest hide outs. Charietto and his gang of goons moved in at night and took their heads in a series of vicious skirmishes. He was rewarded by promotion, eventually becoming *Comes Per Utramque Germanicum*.

Charietto lasted ten years. He was ambushed while leading a small force of comitatenses by a large army of Alamanni. He refused to flee with his cowardly men and died facing the enemy. It is recorded that it took several spear thrusts to bring him down. The Alamanni eluded the magister peditum, Dagalaifus, but were found and destroyed by a strike force of comitatenses commanded by the magister equitum Jovinus.

His scouts followed a trail of burning villas and located the Alamanni camp. It was hidden amongst the trees in a small valley by a river. Jovinus and his men stalked the plunderers while they bathed and dried their hair. Waiting until they were suitably inebriated he sounded the trumpets. The Roman army swept in and won a resounding victory.

Charging Cataphracts

Triumphal parade

INTRODUCTION

The Roman army was not always engaged in epic battles, and long campaigns, in fact a great deal of a soldier's life was spent policing the border. These rules are for fighting small actions between Roman forces and Barbarian raiding parties, or local thugs looking to disturb the tranquil life (all right, not quite tranquil) in the Roman Empire. The following rules modifications are suggested to turn Warhammer Ancient Battles into a skirmish game.

THE RULES

Units/troops

All troops are chosen from the army list. Each model may be independent and may take any actions available to that troop type. Models may group into units, provided there are five or more models of the same type. Units of troops follow the normal rules for units. Characters can lead units.

Independent models may be formed into a unit during the game by moving them together until they touch bases. The models must all be of the same type except that characters can lead a unit. To come together as a unit, models must form up on a model that is (**i**) a character, (**ii**) a musician, or (**iii**) a banner/standard holder.

Movement

Movement is conducted using normal Warhammer Ancient Battles rules.

Shooting

Shooting is carried out as in Warhammer Ancient Battles but remember that all single models are -1 to hit.

Close Combat

Resolve close combat using the Warhammer Ancient Battles rules, except for the special wounding rule below.

Wounding

Once a model loses its last wound it is not necessarily dead. Roll a D6.

D6 Result

1 The model is slightly wounded and stays in the battle but with -1 to all its statistics except Wounds and Attacks which may not fall below 1. If the model is wounded such that it has a WS or BS of zero or less then the model is dead.

4-5 Lay the model on its side, the man is on the ground in agony. At the end of the owning player's turn, roll again.

6 The model drops dead and is removed from the table.

Note that a model on the ground is helpless and at the tender mercies of his opponent (ha!). Any model that is attacked in hand-to-hand combat when on the ground is dead. The attacking player is not obliged to roll any dice, the attack is always lethal. A model must strike an upright enemy that is in base-to-base contact in preference to a stunned opponent – business before pleasure.

Psychology

All tests are taken as usual. The model with the highest Leadership value on each side counts as the General, so any model within 12" may use his Leadership value.

Special Characters

Some leaders excel at the type of combat found in small skirmishes. Examples of such leaders can be found below.

Roman Veteran Campidoctor

A nasty piece of work, likely to frighten his own side as much as the enemy.

	M	WS	BS	S	T	W	I	A	Ld	Pts
Campidoctor	4	4	4	4	3	2	4	2	9	60

Equipment: Sword, light armour, throwing spear and scarred face.

Options: May have large shield (+1 pt), heavy throwing weapon (+1 pt, replaces throwing spear) and may replace light armour with heavy armour (+1 pt).

Special Rules: Any broken troops within 6" automatically rally at the beginning of their turn. *Drilled. Stubborn.*

Roll a D6 at the beginning of the game.

D6	Result
1-2	He causes *fear* in all troops
3-4	He can re-roll any misses in close combat.
5-6	He is lightly wounded on a roll of 1-3 not just 1.

Roman Arcani (O.O.VII.)

Arcani were Rome's answer to James Bond. They were lethal, mendacious and duplicitous – and that was just their good side.

	M	WS	BS	S	T	W	I	A	Ld	Pts
Arcani	5	4	4	4	3	2	5	2	7	60

Equipment: Sword, poisoned wine, cloak and dagger.

Options: May have crossbow concealed in cloak (+3 pts).

Special Rules: May attempt to sneak poisoned bottle of wine into the enemy camp. Roll a D6 for each character starting with the one with the highest Leadership value. On a roll of 1 the model contracts the 'Gaulic Guts' and suffers one wound. Only one character can suffer from the effects of the poisoned wine so stop rolling when you have a victim. The cloak confers a 6+ dodge save that is never modified by an opponent's Strength.

Charietto

One time barbarian, ex bounty hunter, last seen commanding the pride of the Roman army.

	M	WS	BS	S	T	W	I	A	Ld	Pts
Charietto	4	4	4	4	3	2	5	2	7	54

Equipment: Sword, javelin, shield, light armour, and bad attitude.

Options: May have large shield (+1 pt), and heavy throwing weapon (+1 pt, replaces throwing weapon).

Special Rules: Immune to Break and Panic tests. *Infiltration:* He, and any unit that is led by him, may set up hidden in wooded terrain anywhere on the battlefield. The player writes down, or sketches, the position of the hidden unit clearly on a piece of paper. The concealed unit is revealed and placed on the battlefield at the owning player's choice, or when an enemy comes within 6" of the concealing terrain.

Barbarian Thug

This warrior prefers to challenge the enemy to single combat, and excels in one-on-one fights.

	M	WS	BS	S	T	W	I	A	Ld	Pts
Thug	5	4	4	4	3	2	5	2	7	54

Equipment: Sword, throwing weapon and body odour.

Options: May have shield (+1 pt), heavy throwing weapon (+1 pt, replaces throwing weapon) and may have light armour (+3 pts).

Special Rules: Adds +1 to all to hit and to wound rolls in close combat. Immune to Break and Panic tests.

Please note these characters cannot be used in normal games – they will kill anything and everything!

Rome burns

'He who pursues rashly with his forces scattered is willing the adversary the victory he had himself obtained.'

Vegetius

The mobile Western Roman army in the early 5th century, after Tomlin in Connolly, taken from the *Notitia Dignitatum*.

Army	Cavalry	Legions	Aux.	Pseudocomitatenses
Britain	5	2	1	–
Spain	–	5	11	–
Tunisia/Algeria	20	11	1	–
Morocco	3	2	2	–
Gaul	12	5	19	27
Danube	–	6	12	6
Italy	12	13	21	2

Listed below are some of the names of Western units, with associated limitanei, taken from the *Notitia Dignitatum*, after Barker, Holder, and Dobson & Breeze. We have given a greater coverage of the British army for no better reason than we live here!

THE BRITISH ARMY

Comes Britanniae

Comitatenses

Cavalry (Vexillationes)

Equites Scutarii Aureliaci (Shock)
This unit disappears from the records after Britain left the Empire.

Equites Honoriani
Taifali Seniores (Shock)
This unit derived from the Equites Honoriani Seniores and the Equites Taifali. It disappears from the records after Britain left the Empire.

Equites Honoriani Seniores (Shock)
This unit may be the same regiment as the Equites Honoriani Taifali Seniores. It disappears from the records after Britain left the Empire.

Equites Taifali (Shock)
This unit may be the same regiment as the Equites Honoriani Taifali Seniores. It disappears from the records after Britain left the Empire.

Equites Stablesiani (Shock)
This unit was probably promoted to the mobile army from the Equites Stablesiani. Gariannonenses (by Stilicho in 400-402 AD). It disappears from the records after Britain left the Empire.

Equites Syria (Light Bow)
This unit disappears from the records after Britain left the Empire.

Equites Cataphractarii Iuniores (Heavy Armoured Shock)
This unit was probably brought to Britain from the Eastern army in response to barbarian attacks that occurred in 367 AD.

Infantry

Victores Iuniores Britanniciani (Palatine Auxiliary)
This unit was raised by Stilicho in 399-400 AD and based in Britain. It disappears from the records after Britain left the Empire.

Batavi Iuniores Britanniciani (Palatine Auxiliary?)
This unit was raised by Stilicho in 399-400 AD and based in Britain. It was one of the British Expeditionary Force regiments that Constantine III took to Gaul in 407 AD. It never returned and turns up later in the Gaulic army.

Exculcatores Iuniores Britanniciani (Palatine Auxiliary?)
This unit was raised by Stilicho in 399-400 AD and based in Britain. It was one of the British Expeditionary Force regiments that Constantine III took to Gaul in 407 AD. It never returned and turns up later under the command of the magister peditum.

Invicti Iuniores Britanniciani (Palatine Auxiliary?)
This unit was raised by Stilicho in 399-400 AD and based in Britain. It was one of the British Expeditionary Force regiments that Constantine III took to Gaul in 407 AD. It never returned and turns up later in the Spanish army.

Primani Iuniores (Legion)
This unit probably started as a vexillation from the Legio I Adiutrix. It disappears from the records after Britain left the Empire.

Secundani Iuniores (Legion)
This unit probably started as a vexillation from the Legio II Adiutrix. It disappears from the records after Britain left the Empire.

Limitanei

Dux Britanniarum

HADRIAN'S WALL

Cavalry

5 Alae

Infantry

16 Cohortes

1 Numerus

1 Cuneus

THE NORTH

Cavalry

3 Vexillationes

Infantry

1 Legio

10 Numeri

1 Small Unit

Comes Litoris Saxonici (Saxon Shore)

Cavalry

2 Vexillationes

Infantry

1 Legio

3 Numeri

1 Cohors

THE AFRICAN ARMY

1. TUNISIA/ALGERIA

Comes Africae

Comitatenses

Cavalry (Vexillationes)

Equites Scutarii Seniores (Shock)
Equites Scutarii Iuniores
Equites Secundi Scutarii Iuniores
Equites Stablesiani Seniores
Equites Stablesiani Italiciani
Equites Marcomanni
Equites Armigeri Seniores
Equites Armigeri Iuniores
Equites Promoti Iuniores
Equites Honoriani Iuniores
Equites Cetrati Seniores (Light Javelin)
Equites Cetrati Iuniores
Equites Parthi Sagittarii Seniores (Light Bow)
Equites Parthi Sagittarii Iuniores
Equites Sagittarii Clibanarii (Heavy Armoured Bow ?)

Infantry
None

Limitanei

Cavalry
None

Infantry
16 Small Units

2. MOROCCO

Comes Tingitaniae

Comitatenses

Cavalry (Vexillationes)

Equites Scutarii Seniores (Shock)
Equites Cardueni
Equites Sagittarii Seniores (Light Bow)

Infantry
Mauri Tonantes Seniores (Palatine Auxiliary)
Mauri Tonantes Iuniores
Secunda Flavia Constantiniania (Legion)
Septimani Iuniores

Limitanei

Cavalry
1 Ala

Infantry
6 Cohortes

ITALIAN ARMY

The Imperial Bodyguard Units
Schola Scutatorium Prima (Shock Cavalry)
Schola Scutatorium Secunda
Schola Armaturarum Seniorum
Schola Gentilium Seniorum
Schola Scutariorum Tertia
Magister Miletum Intra Italiam
Comitatenses

Cavalry (Vexillationes Palatinae)
Equites Promoti Seniores (shock cavalry)
Equites Brachiati Seniores
Equites Cornuti Seniores
Equites Constantes Valentinianenses Iuniores
Comites Seniores
Comites Alani (Light Bow or Shock)

Cavalry (Vexillationes Comitatenses)
Equites Mauri Feroces (Light Javelin)

Infantry
Iovani Seniores (Palatine Legion)
Herculiani Seniores
Divitenses Seniores
Tungrecani Seniores
Pannoniciani Seniores
Moesiaci Seniores
Octavani
Thebaei
Cornuti Seniores (Palatine Auxiliary)
Cornuti Iuniores
Brachiati Seniores
Celtae Seniores
Heruli Seniores
Batavi Seniores
Mattiaci Seniores
Iovii Seniores
Victores Seniores
Leones Iuniores
Exculcatores Seniores
Grati
Sabini
Felices Iuniores
Atecotti Honoriani Iuniores
Brisigavi Iuniores
Mauri Honoriani Iuniores
Galli Victores
Gratianenses Iuniores
Marcomanni
Mattiari Iuniores (Legion)
Septimani Iuniores
Regii
Germaniciani
Tertia Iulia Alpina
Legio Prima Iulia Alpina (Pseudocomitatenses)
Pontinenses

THE GAULIC ARMY

Magister Equitum Intra Gallas

Comitatenses

Cavalry (Vexillationes Palatinae)

Equites Batavi Seniores (Shock)
Equites Batavi Iuniores
Equites Cornuti Seniores
Equites Brachiati Iuniores

Cavalry (Vexillationes Comitatenses)

Equites Honoriani Seniores (Shock)
Equites Honoriani Taifali Iuniores
Equites Armigeri Seniores
Equites Primi Gallicani
Equites Constantiaci Feroces
Equites Octavo Dalmatae (Light Javelin)
Equites Dalmatae Passerentiacenses
Equites Mauri Alites

Infantry

Lancearii Sabarienses (Palatine Legion)
Mattiaci Iuniores (Palatine Auxiliary)
Mattiaci Iuniores Gallicani
Leones Seniores
Brachiati Iuniores
Salii Seniores
Gratianenses Seniores
Bructeri
Ampsivarii
Valentinianenses Iuniores
Batavi Iuniores
Atecotti Honoriani Seniores
Atecotti Iuniores Gallicani
Iovvii Iuniores Gallicani
Ascarii Honoriani Seniores
Sagittarii Nervii Gallicani (bow armed)
Armigeri Defensores Seniores (Legion)
Lancearii Honoriani Gallicani
Menapii Seniores
Secundani Britones
Ursarienses
Praesidienses
Geminiacenses
Cortoriacenses
Honoriani Felices Gallicani
Martenses Pseudocomitatenses
Abrincateni
Defensores Seniores
Mauri Osismiaci
Legio Prima Flavia Gallicana Constantia
Legio Prima Flavia Martis
Superventores Iuniores
Cornacenses
Legio Septimani Iuniores
Romanenses

THE DANUBE (LIMITANEI)

Dux Raetiae (Upper Danube)

Cavalry

3 Vexillationes
3 Alae

Infantry

Legio III Italica (divided into 5 detachments)
6 Cohortes
1 Milites
1 Gentes

Dux Valeriae (Middle Danube)

Cavalry

14 Vexillationes (Illyrian)
2 Vexillationes (Sagittarii)
1 Vexillatio
2 Cunei (Illyrian)
2 Cunei

Infantry

Legio I Adiutrix (HQ + 5 Cohortes)
Legio II Adiutrix (HQ + 10 Detachments)
6 Cohortes
5 Auxilia

Dux Moesiae Secundae (Lower Danube)

Cavalry

3 Cunei (Illyrian)
4 Cunei

Infantry

Legio I Italica (10 Cohortes)
Legio XI Claudia (10 cohortes)
10 Miletes

Pictish Warlord

·HOW·TO·COLLECT·AN·ARMY·

So you have read the book and, fired with enthusiasm by our breathless prose, are resolved to rush out and buy an army. May we counsel caution, to avoid disappointment some issues need to be resolved first. I would first suggest rereading the sage advice about collecting an army in *Warhammer Ancient Battles*.

SCALE

The first issue to be addressed is what scale figures are you going to select. Wargame models come in a variety of sizes including 25mm, 15mm and 6mm. The most sensible advice is to buy the same scale as the armies collected by your more likely opponents. That way, at least you will have someone to play against.

Wargames models require basing and, in practice, it is the bases that square up against each other in mortal combat, rather than the figures. Warhammer Ancient Battles is remarkably tolerant of base sizing provided all the opposing armies employ the same system. So again, base your figures with potential opponents in mind. Many armies will be on a multiple base system, probably from the Wargames Research Group's popular DBM-WRG 7th Edition rules. This should not present insuperable problems. Just use some method of keeping track of casualties. Personally, we use small coloured dice.

One potential problem is that the Warhammer Ancient Battles rules work best with the sort of unit sizes that are found with 25mm armies. Smaller scales can easily give rise to considerably larger armies and this can lead to some tedious dice rolling. There are two solutions for this. The first is to treat the base as the 'model' for dice rolling purposes, irrespective of the number of figures mounted per base.

The second is to use a one figure per base system, on appropriately smaller bases, but employ the same number of figures as one would with a 25mm army. This can be great fun with 6 mm figures as one ends up with a pocket wargaming army. Some wargamers collect identical 25mm and 6mm pocket armies and use the 6mm as a travel wargaming set, practising tactics in their bedrooms away from the vicissitudes of parents, siblings and the family dog, or taking the set with them to college. Pocket sets are also an excellent way of trying out new units or even whole armies before paying out serious money on 25mm figures. Movement and firing scales have to be adjusted, or small armies unrealistically zip across huge open spaces like Jeremy Clarkson in a new Jag on a frozen lake. Converting inches to centimetres works well for 15mm troops but 6mm need rather more scale compression, inches to quarter inches, for example.

OK, you have decided on a scale and a basing system, now comes the interesting bit. What army are you going to collect? In many ways the Late Roman era gives players more freedom than other periods. You are not straitjacketed by the need to provide your potential opponents a set foe. Everybody in the Late Empire fought everyone else, Romans against Romans and barbarians against barbarians as well as the more traditional Empire takes on all comers.

You will see tasty deals advertised selling whole armies, often at attractive discounts. Tempting as these are, we counsel caution unless you are really, really sure. Even then, we personally find the arrival of a whole box of soldiers through the post somewhat intimidating. Where do you start? How do you set about painting a hundred models? All too often painting becomes a chore, a tedious production line far from the delight that one should experience. Then after a posting to the attic, your army joins the sad ranks of partly painted models at the bring and buy stall. Disaster!

We suggest an alternative strategy to this mournful scenario. If you get the chance, play a few games with someone else's army to get a feel for the period before purchasing. Then start collecting an army by selecting a general. This is the pivotal decision that will govern everything else. What sort of general are you going to be?

Are you a Roman nobleman? Is your blood so blue that you can sign peace treaties by dipping quills in it? Is your upper lip so stiff that you can crack nuts? Was your great, great, great grandfather a personal toady to the divine Julius and have several of your relatives committed suicide after a treason trial? If so you are a 'lantern bearer', holding back the night. One day Rome might disappear, deluged under a sea of bare-bottomed barbarians but not while there is breath in your body. Not while you stand protected by your bodyguard, skilfully moving your well-drilled units around the battlefield to confuse and tear apart unwashed hordes many times their number. Not while your men stand in their disciplined ranks, unlettered but fine lads all of them, real rough diamonds.

Roman Infantryman

On the other hand you could be a barbarian chief. Your great, great grandfather was born in a bog. He became an optimates when he pulled a regales out of said bog. Your great grandfather became a regales when the local king accidentally fell in the bog and someone stood on the back of his head. Your grandfather, who was a younger son, became king in turn when his elder brother died accidentally out hunting after falling on his spear – backwards – three times. You despise those namby, pamby Romans with their poetry readings and central heated villas. Mind you, now you mention it, the old bog gets a bit chilly come Micklemass. Overwintering in a captured Roman villa has its attractions. Another thing, those weakling Roman noblemen standing behind their troops giving orders. March here, march there, poxy dancemasters. A real man stands at the head of his warriors swinging his sword. The only order he needs to give is "CHARGE!"

So choose the right general and spend a little time getting that extra special paint job. This figure is your representative on the battlefield and your troops will not give their best for a sloppy leader. Next start collecting the soldiers one unit at a time. We like to start with a cavalry unit, after all they are the senior service. A Roman cavalry unit from the mobile army consisted of about 250 to 300 men. If we use a 50:1 ratio then a unit will be five to six men. Infantry auxiliaries and legions of about 500 to a 1,000 men will consist of 10 to 20 models. An elite unit will have a leader, *draconarius* and *bucinator*. Barbarian cavalry units would be a similar size to Roman regiments. Warbands could be any size from 500 men (10 models) to 2,500 warriors (50 models).

Buy one unit at a time and finish painting it before buying another. This is so important for maintaining your personal morale. Roman regiments were identified by their shield designs. Some examples are reproduced in this publication, a more comprehensive guide is given by Barker. Do use these designs as guides but, please, do not get anally obsessed by getting the designs 'right'. We have no evidence that the patterns that have come down the years to us are correct. Many of the designs are a bit fiddly and look better simplified. The key point is that all the shields in a regiment should have the same design.

'**N**ow the Roman soldiers, also, had been stationed at the frontiers of Gaul to serve as guards. And the soldiers, having no means of returning to Rome, and at the same time being unwilling to yield to their enemy who were Arians, gave themselves, together with their military standards and the land which they had been guarding for the Romans to the Arborychi and the Germans; and they handed down to their offspring all the customs of their fathers, which were thus preserved, and this people had held them in sufficient reverence to guard them even up to my time. For even at the present day they are clearly recognised as belonging to the legions to which they were assigned when they served in ancient times, and they always carry their own standards when they enter battle, and always follow the customs of their fathers.'

There is no reason why barbarian units should have identical designs but we like to put some sort of 'logo' on all the members of a warband or cavalry unit from a single canton, such as a black cockerel. This is pure fancy on our part but it does seem to give a unit a sense of coherency, and coherent units naturally fight better.

SAMPLE ROMAN ARMY

An example of a 1,000 points Roman army is listed below. It is a small, not very experienced, army of comitatenses, based somewhere in the south-west of Britain.

Characters	.141 pts
Cavalry	.310 pts
Infantry	.585 pts
Total	**.1,036 pts**

CHARACTERS

General (Dux Cornovi Militum) . . . .*141 pts*

We will give him a warhorse (+3 pts) so he can move around the battlefield, and a suit of light armour (+3 pts) for survivability.

CAVALRY

Shock Cavalry (Scutarii) . . . .*120 pts*

Five cavalrymen including a leader (+5 pts), draconarius (+5 pts) and bucinator (+5 pts).

Shock Cavalry (Scutarii) . . . .*120 pts*

Five cavalrymen including a leader (+ 5 pts), draconarius (+5 pts) and bucinator (+5 pts).

Light Cavalry (Equites Dalmatae) . . . .*70 pts*

Five cavalrymen.

INFANTRY

Legion (Cornovi) . . . .*255 pts*

Twenty Pedes including a leader (+ 5 pts), draconarius (+5 pts) and bucinator (+5 pts). The legion is armed with light armour (+2 pts), javelins and darts (+2 pts).

Auxiliary Palatine (Scotii) . . . .*165 pts*

Ten Palantine including a leader (+5 pts), draconarius (+5 pts) and bucinator (+5 pts). The regiment is armed with light armour (+2 pts), and a heavy throwing spear (+1 pt).

Auxiliary Palatine (Caledonii) . . . .*165 pts*

Ten Palantine including a leader (+5 pts), draconarius (+5 pts) and bucinator (+5 pts). The regiment is armed with light armour (+2 pts), and a heavy throwing spear (+1 pt).

SAMPLE BARBARIAN ARMY

A potential opponent for our noble force is the raiding party of Lurkio.

Characters	.235 pts
Cavalry	.130 pts
Infantry	.680 pts
Total	**.1,045 pts**

CHARACTERS

General (Lurkio) – Frankish Warlord . . . . *149 pts*

He has a throwing spear (+2 pts) and a shield (+2 pts).

Optimates (Framio) . . . . *44 pts*

Armed with a warhorse (+3 pts), shield (+1 pt) and throwing spear (+2 pts).

Optimates (Ruguth) . . . . *42 pts*

Armed with shield (+1 pt) and heavy throwing spear (+3 pts).

CAVALRY

Shock Cavalry (Framio's Fast Riders) . . . . *130 pts*

Six warriors. Includes a Musician (+5 pts) and Standard Bearer (+5 pts).

INFANTRY

Warriors (Rugeth's Raiders) . . . . *150 pts*

Twenty warriors armed with heavy throwing spears (+2 pts). Includes a Musician (+5 pts) and Standard Bearer (+5 pts).

Warriors (Lurkio's Lads) . . . . *150 pts*

Twenty warriors armed with heavy throwing spears (+2 pts). Includes a Musician (+5 pts) and Standard Bearer (+5 pts).

Warriors . . . . *165 pts*

Thirty warriors. Includes a Leader (+5 pts), Musician (+5 pts) and Standard Bearer (+5 pts).

Warriors . . . . *165 pts*

Thirty warriors. Includes a Leader (+5 pts), Musician (+5 pts) and Standard Bearer (+5 pts).

Warriors . . . . *50 pts*

Ten warriors, light infantry.

Adding new units can develop a 1,000 points army further. How about some archers for the Roman units, or even a regiment of archers? Roman cavalry might be given more punch by the inclusion of some heavy shock cavalry. The Barbarian army listed above is a Western army. It could be converted into a Central or Eastern army with the addition of some steppe cavalry. The addition of an army standard greatly enhances the look and fighting potential of any army.

Finally a Roman army can be converted into a Warlord army by the addition of a few units of barbarians or a Barbarian army into a Warlord army with a few Roman regiments. Warlord armies are so flexible that they are an easy way to start collecting a new army. If you have enough units you can field a radically different Warlord army every time you play, with new tactics to exploit the novel arrangement. That should make your opponent's life just that little bit more difficult.

Goth nobles lead a charge

·TACTICS·

Welcome to the Tactics section. This is not full of *'win at all costs'* ideas but deals with how to field an army for optimum performance but in a way that reflects the style of warfare at the end the Roman Empire. For the first section we will sneak into a lecture in one of Rome's military colleges for young gentlemen. Armius Tacticus presides…

'All right quiet down in the back there. Zenno, if you do that to Plucitus once more I will be forced to speak to your father. You know what the Senator did last time!

Right, we'll begin.

I will start with Rome's most common troop type – the infantryman. In recent years I feel that our brave pedes have had a bad time of it. The classic legionnaire that carved out our empire 300 years ago is no longer with us but the army should put more faith in the man we have now. Just look at the average fighting soldier. He is equipped with a mail coat, helmet and large shield, enough to protect him from over fifty percent of hits. An attacker must endure a hail of javelins, darts and throwing spears from his ranged weaponry even before they make contact. If the foe closes than our man will cut him down with his side arm. Add to these advantages, high morale and large formations then do you not conclude that we should give the infantry a little more respect!

On the battlefield foot soldiers may take one of two roles – as a heavy or a light infantryman. Firstly the heavy infantrymen. These make up the main battle line. Fielded in close order, these legions form a solid line to base the rest of the army around. The legions should be deployed in deep formations to allow maximum support in close combat. Then, depending on the force you are facing, they can be used defensively or in a more aggressive role. If fighting a mobile force that is fielding superior numbers of cavalry, anchor the legion's exposed flanks to a terrain feature such as a river or rocky outcrop. This stratagem will stop any attempt to turn the vulnerable flanks. Students, I cannot draw your attention strongly enough to the dangers of exposed flanks.

That means you too, Clunkus!

If there are no suitable terrain features, then light infantry and cavalry must suffice. Our infantry is superior to any barbarian in a fair fight but attacks in the flank or rear confuse and dismay our gallant boys.

If the foe facing you is an infantry force, or you are certain they are tactically disadvantaged then here is the opportunity to send your infantry forward (keeping in an ordered line) to hack through the cowards. But always, always make sure nobody gets on your flanks. As a general rule, if your battle plan requires a regiment to stand and take a barbarian charge then be sure to use archers in the rear ranks. Conversely, if a unit is expected to charge the foe then arm the men with heavy javelins.

The light infantryman is used in a much different way. Lightly equip him so not to slow him down, then use smaller formations in roles unsuited to the heavies – operations in difficult ground, holding up the enemy's advance by working around behind them, or disrupting their line by standing in front of them and fleeing when charged. A special mention should be made for archers. If a unit is available, then be sure to use of them. The barbarians have no massed long ranged missiles, so suffer greatly from massed bow fire.

Cavalry are not quite the battle winning force that cavalrymen would have you believe. Yes, they can ride down fleeing skirmishers but as soon as a barbarian warlord turns up with some of his cavalry, your's could be in deep trouble if you're not careful.

Cavalry in battle has two main uses, both of which are related. The first is to attack enemy cavalry and impede them from outflanking your infantry. The second is to outflank the enemy line. The most effective way of achieving this is to have superior numbers of horsemen. This is achieved most simply by bringing along more horses than your foe. Failing that mass your cavalry on one flank whilst defending your other flank using terrain features or light infantry.

Light cavalry have similar objectives but achieve them by different means. Use their speed to move past the enemy and disrupt his force from behind using missiles or by charging vulnerable parts of his army.

A word on cataphracts. These men look fine enough in their armour, riding armoured horses but be careful not to sacrifice another part of your army to include them. Remember, they are very unwieldy and can have circles run round them by almost anything. Cataphracts are best reserved for impressing citizens watching your victory parades, assuming any of you ever have any!

A Roman general's job is to… anyone? Come on, come on… Yes, Furtio? No, stupid boy, not to engage in common fighting. I know what the divine Julius wrote in his memoirs but you shower are far from divine! Save the sword waggling for actors on the stage.

We have far better things to worry about. Place yourself at the middle of the lines, preferably behind the main line in a place of safety and use your authority to boost the men's morale if things start getting sticky. Yes, it might do the men's morale good to see you slaying barbarians, Plotius, but it won't do much for their confidence when some bare-bottomed thug takes your head off with a grass cutter. It only takes a ten denarii spear to waste 20,000 solidi's worth of education. Even if most of the money was wasted in your case, Plotius!

Your other officers should be placed in units outside of your command range to give them a leadership boost. It's alright for younger officers to get stuck in but senior gentlemen should not get involved unless the situation is so bad it would be better to die a hero than have to face Caesar with news of your defeat. Or, if the situation is so good, a well-timed charge could allow you to boast in your report how you personally broke the enemy!'

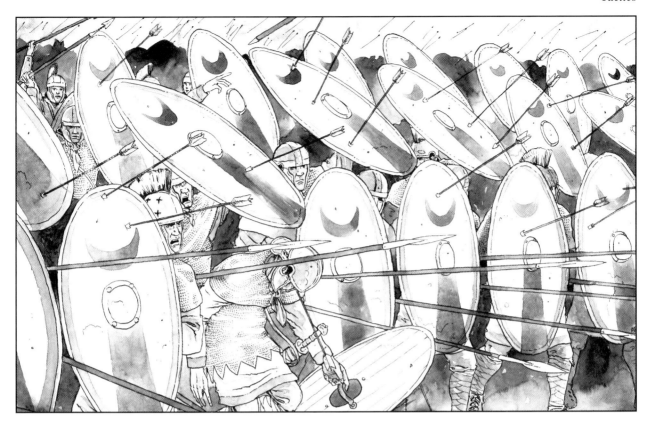

Far away, in the Barbaricum, a chieftain called Brouto has just finished scratching his bum and clearing his throat. Positioning himself on a log, he quaffs deeply of a sour beer and addresses an admiring crowd of young optimates.

'So you want to know how to beat up the Romans, it's easy – just run up to 'em and smack 'em one! But they got ways of stopping us doing that. So here's the best way of doing it, sneaky like.

The biggest part of your warband will be the lads on foot, thousands of them if you are lucky. Use them in a few massive blocks as the lads like to be with their mates and won't run away so easy. As to what to do with them, just run them towards the enemy quick. The longer you hang around, the more arrows will kill the boys, so no dawdling. Anyway, the lads get a bit fired up after a few bevies so they is likely to charge anyhow if you hold them back for too long. Try and get some heavy throwing things for the boys, axes or iron javelins or whatever. Nothing breaks up those tight formations that the girly Romans like to hide in faster than a few throwing axes.

Split off some of the youngsters to form a screen in front of your warbands to stop the missile fire from being too effective, but tell them to run if charged, you don't want them getting all the glory. Watch out for the Roman horsemen. They will try to get behind you so remember to use cavalry if you've got them or send some brave or stupid lads to hold them up. The volunteers from that village you raided last week will do fine!

Blokes on horses are great if you can take some. They will beat up the Roman stuff any day, well most days, but make sure you have plenty. Use them to kill the enemy's horses and then get behind the foot soldiers. If you charge into their backs as the rest of your warriors charge the front then things get really messy dead quick.

Was that you sniggering, Rootio? I would hate to think you was ignoring my pearls of wisdom. I might feel moved to stick this spatha up the rear end of anyone who lacked manners!

The Romans like to use really fast cavalry. So to make sure you get rid of these take a unit of light cavalry to keep them busy. If you've got some lads wearing loads of armour available then take these if you want to look flash but you are better off taking the faster normal stuff. If you're on holiday down south (near the big wall thingys) you will have a lot more cavalry available. In this case, use your infantry to hold the Romans, send in loads of horses to destroy the Roman cavalry and then hit the infantry from all sides.

It's very important to get the lads lined up right at the start. They are not ponsey Romans and will not take kindly to being ordered around in some dance. All they want to do is get stuck in as soon as possible. But be sneaky like. See if you can hide a few in a bog so that they can leap out from behind the Romans.

Right, so you got all the lads where you want them, beat up any who want to argue about it and there is not much else to do except kill stuff. The best place for you is right at the front of the lads in the biggest warband. Put the local regales for each canton in command of his lads and charge forward. Find the Romans who think they are hard and smash them yourself. Your main goal of the day is to get to the Roman boss and split him in two. If you have a senior chief with you put him in the cavalry to add a little bit of backbone.'

So that's it. The most important thing to remember is to get into the spirit of the army and do what you think best, roar your best warcry and may the dice gods be kind.

·NOTES·

NOTE 1 – THE NOTITIA DIGNITATUM

This literally means the List of Positions and is an astonishing document that gives a great deal of information about the Roman army of around 400 AD. The *Notitia* is a civilian and military table of organisation for the Empire. What we now have is not the original, which was lost, but copies of a copy made in 1551 in a monastery at Speyer, Germany. It is a list of units, command appointments, fortresses and factories with their general location.

It shows shield designs for the various regiments. Ammianus Marcellinus recorded that barbarians could identify Roman units by their characteristic shield designs.

It is open to debate how accurate the *Notitia* depictions are. It would be surprising if there had been no corruption of the document in a 1,000 years.

The version we have appears to be the Western copy. Dating is still controversial but it may have been originally prepared on the death of Theodosius for his two sons. The Eastern Empire is probably depicted as it was in 395 AD but the Western lists may have been partially updated until about 420 AD or 430 AD. Different Western sections of the Notitia may have different dates, which may explain why some units are in two places at once.

NOTE 2 – THE HISTORY OF THE DECLINE AND FALL OF THE ROMAN EMPIRE, EDWARD GIBBON

'Another damned, thick, square, book! Always scribble, scribble, scribble! Eh! Mr Gibbon?'

The Duke of Gloucester, 1781

From 1776 to 1788, an English historian published his six volume work of scholarship on the fall of the Western Empire. This work has become the most famous single work of a historian in the English language; it still repays reading two centuries on. It is *'a bridge that carried one from the ancient world to the modern.'* (Madame Necker).

Gibbon was born in Putney in the county of Surrey on the 8th May, 1737, the eldest son of a well-to-do family. He was named after his father and lost his mother in childbirth. He had six siblings. In poor health, he spent much of his time convalescing indoors, reading. At fifteen, this studious youth was sent to Magdalen College, Oxford to obtain an education.

Roman Officer

A rebellious student, he shocked his family by converting to Roman Catholicism. His outraged father was obliged to send him to a Calvinist minister in Lausanne for deprogramming. Gibbon completed his education there, fell in love and was recalled to England by his exasperated pater in 1758. From 1760 to 1762 he joined the Militia to protect England against the French.

In 1763, Gibbon went on a 22 month Grand Tour of Europe, including Italy. He explains *'It was at Rome, on the 15th of October 1764 as I sat musing amid the ruins of the capital… that the idea of writing (his history) first started to my mind'*

Gibbon intended to narrate *'the triumph of barbarism and religion'*. He saw the study of history as *'the register of the crimes and follies and misfortunes of mankind'*. He noted that *'of every reader, the attention will be excited by an History of the Decline and Fall of the Roman Empire; the greatest, perhaps, and the most awful scene in the history of mankind'*. The mighty work took 20 years to complete.

Gibbon's history opens in the second century. His most famous quote is the opening statement that *'If a man were called to fix the period in the history of the world during which the condition of the human race was most happy and prosperous, he would, without hesitation, name that which elapsed from [96 AD to 180 AD]'*. The great historian set the start of the decline with the policies of the Emperor Septimus Severus, AD 193-211. Severus stripped away the veil of pretence that the Roman Republic still existed and ruled by naked military power.

Gibbon catalogued the decline of Roman civilisation in literature, art, philosophy and architecture until *'the Roman world was overwhelmed by a deluge of barbarians'*.

NOTE 3 – THE PROVINCES OF BRITAIN

'Britain, you are indeed fortunate… Nature, rightly endowed you with every benefit of land and climate… While the night and its constellations revolve, the sun himself, who to us appears to go down, in Britain seems only to go past.'

Panegyric to Constantine, who was crowned at York.

Britain was a frontier province in every sense of the word. Its geographic position in the 'world-ocean' beyond the Mediterranean made it foreign to the Roman mind in a way that, say, Spain was not. Here, Roman culture failed first and failed completely; Latin rapidly became a dead language. All of Britain was frontier in the sense that nowhere was out of range of sea raiders.

In 350 AD, the Roman part of Britain, which included everything south of Hadrian's Wall, was divided into four provinces. The north of Britain consisted of *Britannia Secunda* and *Flavia Caesariensis* with capitals at York and Lincoln. *Britannia Prima* lay in the West with a capital at Cirencester and the Home Counties lay in the province of *Maxima Caesiensis* with London as its capital.

Each province had a governor (*praeses* or *consularis*) but the vicarius, who was the senior civilian administrator, had his palace and staff in London. The *Notitia Dignitatum* lists three other senior military positions; the *Comes Britanniae* who commanded the British Comitatenses, the *Dux Britanniarum* who commanded the limitanei on Hadrian's Wall and the north and the *Comes Litoris Saxonici per Britannias* who commanded the limitanei in the Saxon Shore forts of the east and south coasts.

The threat to Roman Britain came mostly from the seas that surrounded it. From Denmark and the north-west German coast, Germanic barbarians, Saxons, Angles and Jutes, raided the eastern and south coasts. From Ireland, Celtic barbarians attacked the entire western and south-western coastline. Celtic Picts sailed from Scotland down the north-east coast and occasionally climbed over the Wall.

These threats caused the Romans to build a series of fortifications. There was the Wall itself and a whole series of small forts and signal stations around the coasts. On the east and south coasts the mighty Saxon Shore forts guarded key points and provided bases for anti-pirate fleets. Walls defended cities and many towns and small forts were built along the roads.

In 342 AD, the Emperor Constans had to make an emergency winter voyage to Britain, a hazardous undertaking, for some reason connected with the *arcani*. The fort at Pevensey was built at this time. A few years later the Comes Gratian was despatched to Britain for another emergency. While Julian was campaigning in Gaul in 360 AD, Picts invaded the province so he sent Lupicinus, one of his generals, to restore the situation.

A major collapse occurred in 367 AD. Part of the army in Britain, under a commander called Valentinus, colluded with the arcani and the barbarians. Britain was overrun with gangs of marauding Picts and Scots. The *Comes Litoris Saxonici* (*Nectaridus*) was killed and the *Dux Britanniarum* (*Fullofaudes*) captured. Theodosius, father of the later emperor of the same name, landed at Richborough with reinforcements and advanced on London. He broke his

army into pursuit units that eliminated the bands of barbarians and relieved them of their ill-gotten spoils.

Quickly regaining control of the situation, he pardoned deserters and leaving Britain in the hands of the civilian authorities mounted a campaign into the Barbaricum in 368 AD. Valentinus openly revolted and was executed and the arcani were disbanded. Theodosius 'restored the cities and forts'; a complete reorganisation of British defences was carried out. The four provinces were combined into a single province called *Valentia*. Londinium was renamed *Augusta* in celebration of its loyalty but we may surmise that the locals continued with the old name.

In this period, the forts north of the Wall were abandoned, Roman civilisation was winding down in Britain. Villas and towns were falling into disrepair. In 379 AD when Thedosius obtained the purple, Magnus Maximus, a Spanish general who had fought with Theodosius' father in Britain, was sent to the province. He fought a campaign against the Picts in 382 AD and completely reorganised the defences, including moving barbarian allies to guard the Welsh coastline. The kings of Dyfed in Wales claimed legitimacy from Maximus. Maximus revolted in 383 AD and crossed to Gaul with the British mobile army.

In 398 AD the Picts raided south again. This time the Empire sent Stilicho who suppressed the problem by 399 AD. There was a last round of fortification. The river defences in London were erected at this time. This was the last time that the Empire sent an expeditionary force to Britain. The post of Comes Britanniae was created with a small mobile army and he was supposed to supply the necessary strategic reserves in the future. In 401 AD, Stilicho ran down the British defences by withdrawing a legion from the Wall. The defence of Britain was becoming a luxury the Empire could ill afford.

Goth warrior

The pace now speeds up. At the end of 406 AD the barbarians crossed the Rhine and moved quickly to the coast of Gaul isolating Britain from the Imperial administration. The same year the army in Britain rebelled and appointed their own Emperor, Marcus, possibly these events were related. In early 407 AD, Marcus was killed and replaced by Gratian, a town councillor. He lasted a couple of months before being assassinated and replaced by an army commander, Constantine. This story was brilliantly fictionalised by Alfred Duggan in *The Little Emperors*. Constantine crossed to Gaul with the Comitatenses almost immediately. Like Maximus, he never returned.

In 408 AD, a devastating Saxon raid smashed the depleted defence of the province. There was another revolt and Roman administrators (Constantine's administrators?) were expelled. The British pushed back the Saxons and liberated the cities. Bacaudae uprisings were taking place across the Western parts of Gaul and the Romans viewed the British uprisings in the same light. However, bacaudae were more likely to join barbarians than expel them so it is all a bit of a mystery.

Even more astonishingly, the British, or some British cities, made an appeal for help to Honarius in 410 AD as more barbarian raids developed. He recommended that they look to their own defence. The year 410 AD is usually regarded as the end of the Roman Empire in the British Isles. It was also the year St Patrick was born in Britain.

The Bishop St Germanus visited Britain in 428 AD and again in the 440s AD to combat heresy. He met various officials and clergymen suggesting that Roman life was continuing in some form. The archaeological evidence shows a general trend of a collapse of town life and a move to refortifying the old Celtic hill forts.

It is likely that the continuing military crisis would throw up military leaders who would take power from the city councils. One such man was Vortigern (Celtic for high king) who may have been born in about 360 AD. The legend is that Vortigern settled Saxons in Kent as allies under Hengest and Horsa. These allies rebelled and the Gaulic chroniclers recorded that Britain, or at least the south-east coast, passed into Saxon hands.

The legends also record a battle at about this time between two factions of British at Wallop. The losers were led by Vortimer and are associated with the pro-Saxon faction. Ambrosius Aurelius who claimed descent from emperors and is associated with a pro-Roman party led the winners.

In 470 AD, a British army under Riothamus (another Celtic title rather than name) was invited to settle in Armorica, henceforth called Brittany, as a counterweight to the Visigoths. Ambrosius fought a series of skirmishes with the Saxons and their British allies culminating in the decisive British victory at Badon Hill, around 500 AD. This battle is associated with a shadowy British hero whose story will be told in another supplement.

Roman engineers ford a river

NOTE 4 – AMMIANUS MARCELLINUS (AD 330 – 395), SOLDIER & SCHOLAR

'It is not without the most sincere regret that I must now take leave of an accurate and faithful guide'

Gibbon

Ammianus was one of the greatest Roman historians. Only part of his history has survived, Books 14-31 covering the years 354 AD to 378 AD. For most of the text, modern historians have to rely on a single 9th century manuscript complete with corruptions and omissions. Nevertheless, this work gives an exciting window into military affairs in the Late Roman Empire.

The history appears to have been written in the 380s AD and 390s AD. A letter from Libanius in 392 AD praises some early books and urges Ammianus to finish more. One problem is that ancient historians thought of themselves as artists so the account is full of literary devices. These can be extremely irritating when it comes to reconstructing tactics, formations and equipment.

Ammianus was born into a wealthy family that lived in the great city of Antioch on the Orontes, the capital of Roman Syria, in 330 AD. Antioch, 'the jewel of the east', was an important cultural and governmental centre of a rich, civilised province. The local language was Syriac but the ruling classes, to which Ammianus belonged, spoke Greek. He received an education appropriate for his class.

In his early 20s, he was appointed a *protector domesticus*, a member of an elite corps of staff officers that served the emperor and his commanders. This appointment indicates that Ammianus' family had power and influence. We may thank the patron saint of wargamers that he chose to go into the army rather than the civil service.

Ammianus was appointed to the staff of Urcinus in 354 AD. Urcinus lost his position and was recalled soon afterwards. Ammianus with commendable loyalty followed his general. In 355 AD, Urcinus and Ammianus were sent on a secret mission to murder the Gaulic usurper Silvanus and Julian was given command of Gaul. The two intriguers stayed with the future emperor as he campaigned on the Rhine.

Urcinus regained his command in the east in 357 AD and, again, Ammianus followed him. Then the Persians invaded Roman Mesopotamia in 359 AD. Ammianus was in the thick of the action, escaping from the siege and sack of Amida in the final death agony of the fortified city.

In 363 AD, he joined the Emperor Julian's disastrous Persian expedition. He accompanied the army down the Euphrates. Ammianus was among the officers who appointed Jovian, a senior corps commander and son of a famous general, Emperor. Ammianus, however, never forgave Jovian for his humiliating concessions to the Persians. The historian left the army and returned to Antioch, surviving the treason trials in the city of 371 AD by the expedient of burning his library.

Soon afterwards he moved to Rome. In the eyes of Ammianus' class of person, Rome was the centre of civilisation. In 384 AD foreigners, including Ammianus, were expelled from the city to alleviate a food shortage, although this ruling did not affect dancing girls! Ammianus was forever indignant that dancers had higher status than scholars in Roman society (some things never change! JL). The next few years saw the start of religious intolerance against the pagans. His first books were published in 390 AD or 391 AD, possibly the last ones between 392 AD and the death of Theodosius. Ammianus, himself, died in 395 AD.

NOTE 5 – SOME USEFUL NAMES

It can be very satisfying to personalise one's collection of units by naming their leaders and following their fortunes from battle to battle. The reader should consult page 94 of *Warhammer Ancient Battles*. Names of famous people are scattered through this book but some additional names are listed below.

ROMAN	BARBARIAN
Ampio	Abruna
Avitianus	Bantio
Cascinivus	Buraido
Dassiolus	Derdio
Emeterius	Evingus
Fortunatus	Flainus
Gennadius	Gainas
Ianuarinus	Hariso
Iovianus	Ilateuta
Lycianus	Manio
Maritus	Mundilo
Memorius	Natuspardo
Olympius	Odiscus
Plaianus	Perula
Roveos	Sanbatis
Salvius	Sindila
Taulas	Totila

Roman Infantry

BRITISH LIMITANEI UNITS IN ABOUT 400 AD

Name	First Recorded in Britain (AD)	Location in approx. 400 AD and notes
Legio II Augusta	43	Richborough (part of original invasion force under Vespasian)
Legio VI Victrix	122	York (dates back to the Republic)
Ala II Asturum	122	Chesters (originated from north-west Spain)
Ala Augusta Gallorum Petriana milliaria civium Romanum	98	Stanwix (T. Pomponius Petra – famous commander of the regiment
Ala Herculea	297	Elslack (raised by Maximian, 295-305 AD, brought to Britain by Constantius Chlorus)
Ala I Hispanorum Asturum	98 (?43)	Benwell (originated from north-west Spain, possibly part of original invasion force under Vespasian)
Ala I Pannoniorum Sabiniana	122	Haltonchesters (originated in Hungary)
Cohors I Asturum eq.		Greatchesters (originated from north-west Spain)
Cohors I Baetasiorum CR ob virtutem et fidem	103	Reculver
Cohors I Batavorum eq.	122	Carrawburgh (May have fought at Mons Graupius)
Cohors I Aelia classica	146	Tunnocelum (Burrow walls?) – raised from sailors
Cohors I Cornoviorum		The only British foederati unit. Possibly raised by Hadrian from a tribe in Shropshire. The 'Corn' in the name is also associated with Cornwall in the Dark Ages. Arguably, this makes the Duke of Cornwall's and the Shropshire Light Infantry the oldest regiments in the British Army
Cohors I Aelia Dacorum milliaria		Birdoswald (raised by Hadrian in Dacia and sent immediately to Britain where it helped build the wall)
Cohors II Delmatarum eq.	43	Carvoran
Cohors I Frisiavonum	105	Rudchester (raised in lower Germany after the Civilis revolt)
Cohors I Frixagorum		Rudchester (may be the same as the above regiment)
Cohors III Gallorum eq.	122	Vindolanda (fort on the Stanegate)
Cohors I Hispanorum eq.	98	Bowness
Cohors I Aelia Hispanorum milliaria eq.	119	Axelodonum (raised by Hadrian, it built the fort at Maryport)
Cohors II Lingonum eq.	98	Drumburgh
Cohors III Lingonum eq.	122	Wallsend
Cohors I Morimorum et Cersiacorum	103	Ravenglass (raised from two tribes in Boulogne)
Cohors II Thracum eq.	103	Moresby (raised in Thrace in 26 AD)
Cohors I Tungrorum milliaria	146	Housesteads (raised from the Tungri of Belgium after the Civilis revolt, fought at Mons Graupius)
Cohors II Tungrorum milliaria eq. CL		Castlesteads (raised from Tungri of Belgium after the Civilis revolt)
Cuneus Sarmatarum (numerus Sarmatarum Bremetennacensium)	175	Ribchester (formed from some of the 5,500 Sarmatians sent to Britain in 175 AD by Marcus Aurelias)
Numerus Exploratorum		Bowes
Numerus Exploratorum Bremeniensium		Portchester
Numerus Exploratorum Habitancensium		Portchester (may be same as above)
Numerus Maororum Aurelianorum	253	Burgh-by-Sands (raised from the Moors of Africa)
Equites Cataphractarii		Morbium (Piercebridge)
Equites Dalmatae		Praesidium (raised by Gallienus, 260-268 AD)
Equites Dalmatae Branodunenses		Brancaster
Equites Crispiani		Danum (Doncaster?)
Equites Stablesiani Garionnonenses		Burgh Castle
Milites Tungrecani	367	Dover (sent to Britain after the great barbarian raid of 367 AD, demoted from field army as punishment after backing the usurper Procopius in 365 AD)
Numerus Abulcorum	351	Pevensey (moved to mobile army of Gaul in the early 5th century)
Numerus Defensorum	367	Kirkby Thore (part of Theodosian relief force after raids in 367 AD)
Numerus Directorum		Brough-under-Stainmore
Numerus Fortensium		Bradwell (This unit started as vexillation from the legio II Traiana)
Numerus Longovicianorum		Lanchester
Numerus Nerviorum Dictensium		Dictis (Wearmouth?) – arrived in Britain as a vexillation of the Nervii Seniores with the Theodosian relief force after 367 AD
Numerus Pacensium		Magis (Old Carlisle?) – arrived in Britain as a vexillation of the Legio I Flavia Pacis with the Theodosian relief force after 367 AD
Numerus Solensium		Maglone (Old Carlisle?) – arrived in Britain as a vexillation of the Solenses Seniores with the Theodosian relief force after 367 AD
Numerus Supervenientium Petueriensium		Malton (originally a nautical unit at Brough-on-Humber using ships called pictae)
Numerus Turnacensium		Lympne – arrived with Theodosian relief force after 367 AD
Numerus vigilum		Chester-le-Street

THE ROMAN EMPIRE AT THE BEGINNING OF THE 5th CENTURY

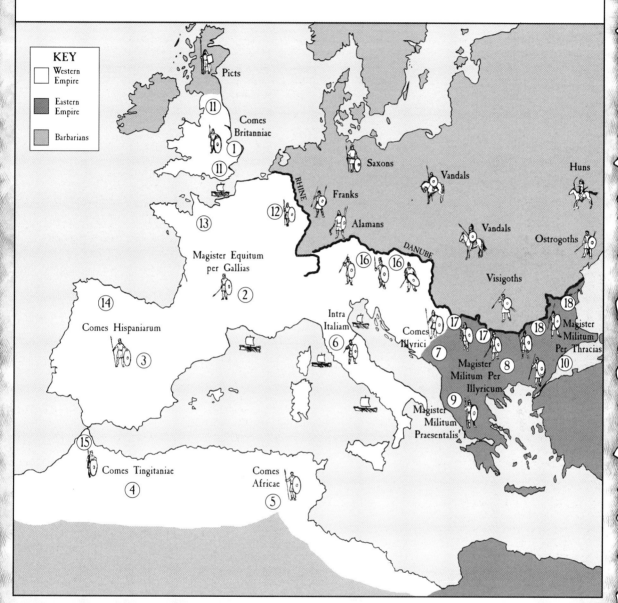

KEY
- Western Empire
- Eastern Empire
- Barbarians

Picts

Comes Britanniae

Saxons

Vandals

Huns

Franks

Alamans

Vandals

Ostrogoths

Magister Equitum per Gallias

Visigoths

RHINE

DANUBE

Intra Italiam

Magister Militum Per Thracias

Comes Illyrici

Comes Hispaniarum

Magister Militum Per Illyricum

Magister Militum Praesentalis

Comes Tingitaniae

Comes Africae

The Numbers of Troops in Field Armies

	Infantry	Cavalry		Infantry	Cavalry
1)	2,000	3,000	6)	23,000	3,500
2)	26,500	4,000	7)	6,500	7,000
3)	10,500	–	8)	16,500	1,000
4)	3,000	1,500	9)	15,000	6,000
5)	10,500	9,500	10)	20,000	3,500

The Numbers of Frontier Troops (Limitanei)

	Infantry	Cavalry		Infantry	Cavalry
11)	19,000	5,000	15)	3,500	500
12)	6,000	–	16)	77,000	22,500
13)	6,000	–	17)	32,000	12,500
14)	6,000	–	18)	50,000	22,000

Notes: Flotillas sailed all along the Danube as well as places marked with ships.

Where two of the same number are used this represents the amount of troops distributed between the two numbers.

A SMALL ROMAN FIELD FORCE

Below is an infantry auxilia with an accompanying cavalry arm. An auxilia was 500-600 strong, made up of three ordines each of two centurise. Cavalry vexillatis were 300 strong and divided into three ordines.

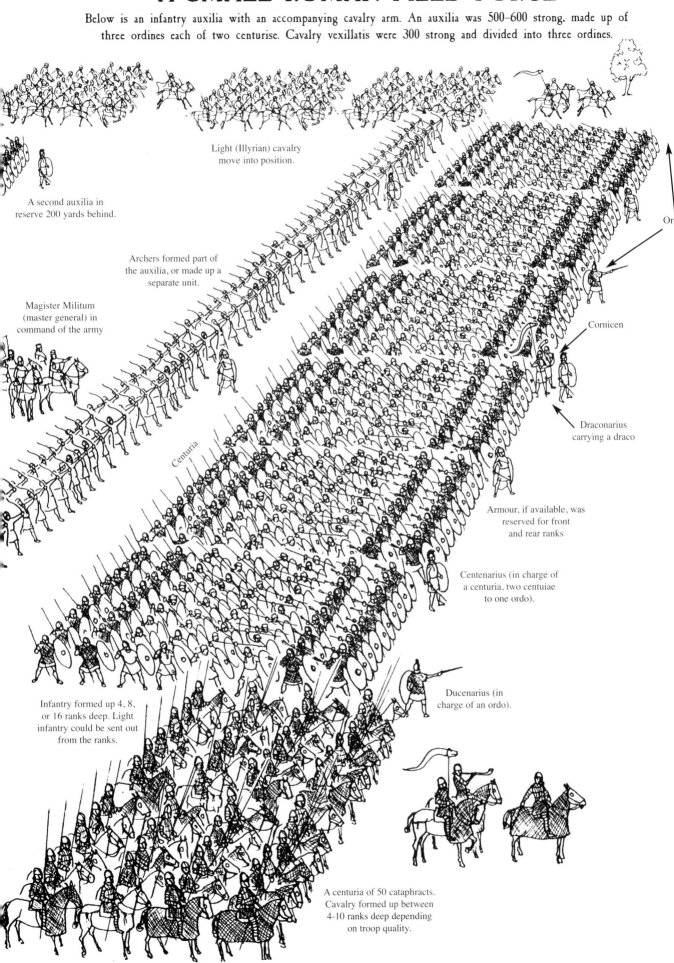

Light (Illyrian) cavalry move into position.

A second auxilia in reserve 200 yards behind.

Archers formed part of the auxilia, or made up a separate unit.

Magister Militum (master general) in command of the army

Centuria

Ord

Cornicen

Draconarius carrying a draco

Armour, if available, was reserved for front and rear ranks

Centenarius (in charge of a centuria, two centuiae to one ordo).

Infantry formed up 4, 8, or 16 ranks deep. Light infantry could be sent out from the ranks.

Ducenarius (in charge of an ordo).

A centuria of 50 cataphracts. Cavalry formed up between 4-10 ranks deep depending on troop quality.

AN ALAMANNIC WAR PARTY

A small army made up of three comitatus plus cavalry. A comitatus or warband could be made up of anything between 100–300 men.

Franks and Alammani made the most of cover for ambushing

Normal warriors

Lower status warriors

A chief or noble picked to lead the comitatus

More nobles

The boar's head (or cuneus) was the typical German attack formation

The nobles in the front ranks were better armoured and armed, ie, with angons and francisca (throwing axes)

Alamannic cavalry, mainly noble

Warlord

Again adopting a cunus formation some of the cavalry hold their shields high over their horse's necks, a style adopted by the Romans

FURTHER INFORMATION

This is not a complete list of the references used in producing this book but it does include those that are readily and cheaply available, usually in paperback, that are likely to be of interest to wargamers. Elton is highly recommended as a manual to Late Roman warfare in Europe. Available in an inexpensive paperback this is the most modern and definitive work on warfare in the Late Western Empire. It gives a comprehensive breakdown of Roman and Barbarian organisation, tactics, weaponry and troop types. The book is derived from Elton's Oxford D.Phil. (1990). It has been a primary source of information for troop types, organisation and tactics. Ferrill has an excellent account of the historical military events, including the great battles. He has been a major source for us.

Osprey books are always invaluable sources of modelling ideas for wargamers but we draw the reader's attention specifically to the recent work by MacDowall, which is quite superb.

Barker's writing needs no introduction from us; he is always a well of inspiration. This study is the best source of *Notitia* information to which the average wargamer is likely to have access. Connolly's book should be on every ancient wargamer's shelves, at the time of writing it has just been reprinted.

Finally, we would urge you to read the words of Marcellinus. We hope the few extracts published here convince you that nothing else can give such an evocative feel for the era. A paperback edition is available from Penguin.

HISTORY BOOKS

Elton, H (1997) *Warfare in Roman Europe AD 350-425*. Oxford Classical Monographs, Clarendon Press, Oxford. 312pp.

Ferrill, A (1983) *The Fall of the Roman Empire – The Military Explanation*. Thames & Hudson, London. 192pp.

Johnson, S (1980) *Later Roman Britain – Britain before the Conquest*. Book Club Associates, London. 195pp.

Starr, CG (1982) *The Roman Empire*. Oxford University Press, New York. 206pp.

OSPREY BOOKS

MacDowall, S (1994) *Late Roman Infantryman, AD 236-565*. Warrior Series. No.9 London. 64pp.

MacDowall, S (1995) *Late Roman Cavalryman, AD 236-565*. Warrior Series. No. 15 London. 64pp.

Nicolle, D (1984) *Arthur and the Anglo-Saxon wars*. Men At Arms Series. No. 154. London. 40pp.

Nicolle, D (1990) *Attila and the Nomad Hordes*. Elite Series. No. 30. London. 64pp.

Roman Junior Officer

Simpkins, M (1979) *The Roman Army from Hadrian to Constantine*. Men At Arms Series. No. 93. London. 40pp.

Wilcox, P (1982) *Rome's Enemies: Germanics and Dacians*. Men At Arms Series No. 129. London. 40pp.

Wilcox, P (1985) *Rome's Enemies (2): Gallic and British Celts*. Men At Arms Series No. 158. London. 48pp.

WARGAMING BOOKS

Barker, P (1981) *Armies and Enemies of Imperial Rome*. WRG Publication. Worthing. 145pp.

Connolly, P (1981) *Greece and Rome at war*. Macdonald Phoebus, London. 320pp.

Johnson, J, Priestley, R, Perry, A & Perry, M (1998) *Warhammer Ancient Battles*. Warhammer Historical Wargames, Nottingham. 144pp.

MacDowall, S (1990) *Wargaming in History: Romans, Goths & Huns*. Argus Books, UK. 95pp.

Newark, T (1985) *The Barbarians*. Blandford Press, London. 144pp.

Newark, T (1986) *Celtic Warlords*. Blandford Press, London. 144pp.

Newark, T (1987) *Medieval Warlords*. Blandford Press, London. 144pp.

Tomlin, R (1989) *The Late Roman Empire*. In (J Hacket, ed.) Warfare in the Ancient World. Sidgwick & Jackson, London. p. 222-249.

CLASSICAL WORKS

Gibbon, E (1776-1778) *The Decline and Fall of the Roman Empire*.

Hamilton, W (1986) Ammianus Marcellinus – *The Later Roman Empire*. Penguin Classics. London. 506pp.

FICTION

Breem, A *Eagle in the Snow*.

Duggan, A *The Little Emperors*.

Roberts, K *The Book of Fate*.

Sutcliffe, R *Sword at Sunset*.

Sutcliffe, R *The Lantern Bearers*.

MAGAZINES

Most of these magazines cover wargames in general, rather than ancient wargaming specifically, but they are none the worse for that! Note that many of these magazines are available in your local newsagents.

Wargames Illustrated, 18 Lovers Lane, Newark, Notts, NG24 1HZ, England

Published and edited by the irrepressible Duncan Macfarlane, Wargames Illustrated easily has the sexiest photos of toy soldiers in any wargames magazine!

Miniature Wargames, Pireme Publishing Ltd, Suite 10, Wessex House, St Leonard's Road, Bournemouth, BH8 8QS

MWAN, 22554 Pleasant Drive, Richton Park, IL 60471, USA (available in the UK from Caviler Books, 816-818 London Road, Leigh-On-Sea, Essex SS9 3NH)

MWAN is very much a labour of love, published every two months by its hard working editor and publisher Hal Thinglum. While not as glossy as many of the other magazines listed here, Hal's sheer enthusiasm and love of the hobby shines through on every page, making this one of the very best wargames magazines around.

Saga, 890 Janes Road, Rochester, New York 14612, USA

Unlike the magazines listed above, Saga is dedicated only to ancient and medieval wargaming.

White Dwarf, Games Workshop Mail Order, Willow Road, Lenton, Nottingham, NG7 2WS, England, Tel: (0115) 91 40000

White Dwarf only covers science-fiction and fantasy wargaming, but it has lots of articles useful for any wargamer, not to mention frequently featuring articles penned by the authors of these rules!

MANUFACTURERS & PUBLISHERS

Wargames Foundry, The Foundry Ltd, 24-34 St. Marks Street, Nottingham NG3 1DE. Tel. 0115 8413000 (available in the USA from The Foundry Ltd, 1549 Marview Drive, Westlake, Ohio 44145, USA). Website: www.wargamesfoundry.com

Essex Miniatures, Unit 1, Shannon Square, Thames Estuary Estate, Canvey Island, Essex SS8 0PE

Alan Warrior

Further Information

Miniature Figurines Ltd, 1-5 Graham Road, Southampton, SO14 0AX, England

Old Glory Miniatures, Box 20, Calumet, PA 15621 USA (available in the UK from Institute House, New Kyo, Stanley, Co. Durham, DH9 7TJ)

Gripping Beast, 19 Woodville Road, Ipswich, Suffolk IPA 1PA

Monolith Designs (for buildings), 'Jamarco', Strawberry Gardens, Hornsea, Hull, East Yorkshire HU18 1US. Website: www.monolith.karoo.net

Wargames Research Group, The Keep, Le Marchant Barracks, London Road, Devizes, Wiltshire SN10 2ER, England
WRG have been keeping the light of ancient wargaming burning for a quarter of a century, and publishes a wide range of rules and reference books on the subject. The Warhammer rules owe a huge debt to WRG's pioneering work over the years.

Osprey, Osprey Military Messenger, PO Box 5, Rushden, Northants NN10 6YX, England
Osprey publish a huge range of reference books on all periods of military history. You can get on their mailing list by writing to the above address.

Caliver Books, Caviler Books, 816-818 London Road, Leigh-On-Sea, Essex SS9 3NH
Caliver carry a wide range of books and rules by numerous publishers.

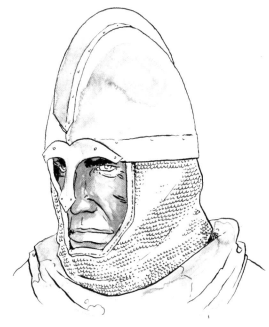

Roman Officer

SOCIETIES

The Society of Ancients, The Membership Secretary, Mabar, Blackheath Lane, Wonersh, Guildford, Surrey GU5 0ON
If you're seriously into ancient wargaming then you really should be a member of the SOA. Their bi-monthly magazine, Slingshot, is a gold-mine of ideas and inspiration!

Warhammer Players Society, 40 Summers Mead, Brimsham Park, Yate, Bristol BS37 7RB
Website: www.players-society.com
Need to find opponents near you then this is the place. Also check out their website for information on events and tournaments using the Warhammer Ancient Battles rules.

The Solo Wargamers Association, Membership Secretary, 120 Great Stone Road, Firswood, Manchester, M16 0HD
Can't find an opponent? Then the Solo Wargamers Association is for you!

ACKNOWLEDGMENTS

Many people have made this work possible. The authors would like to single out Jervis Johnson, without whose enthusiasm and encouragement it would never have been written. We must thank Dr Elton for helpful discussion and correcting some of our wilder ideas, but he must not be blamed for any remaining inaccuracies. We acknowledge the importance of the playtesting and development advice received from Steve Row, and others at Games Workshop and various Kent wargames clubs.

Finally, can we thank all those whose ideas have been such an influence to us over the years, Charles Grant, Donald Featherstone, Greg Pitts, John Southard and all the wargame designers at WRG and Games Workshop.

Frankish Warrior